Aggression on the road

Aggression on the road

A PILOT STUDY OF BEHAVIOUR IN THE DRIVING SITUATION

MEYER H. PARRY, M.A.

Department of Psychology,
University of Strathclyde, Glasgow

TAVISTOCK PUBLICATIONS
LONDON NEW YORK SYDNEY TORONTO WELLINGTON

First published in 1968
by Tavistock Publications Limited
11 New Fetter Lane, London EC4
Printed in Great Britain
In 10 pt 'Monotype' Plantin 2 pts leaded
By Richard Clay (The Chaucer Press), Ltd.,
Bungay, Suffolk
© *Meyer H. Parry 1968*

Distributed in the USA
by Barnes & Noble, Inc.

To Sandy in appreciation
To Kate, my daughter,
in resignation!

Contents

List of figures

Acknowledgements

Chiefly, I owe my thanks to the many people, mainly motorists, who agreed to take part in this survey. For their participation and full co-operation I am very grateful.

Special mention must be made of the following to whom I am indebted:

The publications department of the Road Research Laboratories for permission to quote extracts from *Research on Road Safety* (1963), and to the library staff of the Road Research Laboratories for their assistance.

To Dr Gordon Claridge and the British Broadcasting Corporation for permission to quote from *Motoring and the Motorist*.

Thanks are also due to the Director and Staff of the Public Library, Haringey, London, for their co-operation in distributing questionnaires through the library facilities and for their assistance in seeking relevant literature.

Special thanks to Sumlock Comptometers for their very generous loan of the Anita, a machine which proved to be invaluable for streamlining calculations.

Also to those inspectors and officers of the Traffic Division, Metropolitan Police, London, who gave up some of their very valuable time to answer queries.

To those members of insurance companies and Ministry of Transport driving examiners for their assistance.

To Michael Mayers for helpful criticism.

Finally, to my wife, for her co-operation, enthusiasm, and encouragement.

M. H. P.

Preface

There is little doubt that however general the area of research, the task of studying the behaviour of motorists while driving, with a view to establishing which 'types' are more accident-prone than others, is an extremely difficult one. Immediately, one is obliged to answer satisfactorily the following points:

(*i*) What is meant by 'types', and how does one effectively classify them?

(*ii*) What is 'accident-proneness'?

The term 'types' usually refers to a group or groups of people showing significantly similar patterns of the variable being measured or investigated.

In attempting to define accident-proneness, the assumption is made that the individual's tendency to be involved in an accident is due either to the laws of chance or to an inherent capacity to have accidents. In order to use these definitions as an effective yardstick against which to measure the degree of accident-proneness, it would first become necessary to have, and to keep, up-to-date records of accidents, similar to those kept in, for example, factories.

To do this would be to achieve the impossible, since it would involve categorizing and separating motor accidents into those precipitated by some known and measurable 'human' weakness and those brought about by chance situations. The very fact that the motoring environment of each driver differs* (in some instances rather widely) makes any attempt of categorization even more unrealistic.

For example, some drive large vehicles, others small; some drive regularly, others only occasionally; some drive out in the country, others mainly in towns; some drive large distances daily, others only a few miles a day, and so on. Where there is so much variation, the task of defining 'accident-proneness' is soluble only as a term relative within the framework of a specific study or research programme.

---

* No differentiation has been made for the terms 'driver' and 'motorist' in this investigation. Both indicate a person responsible for taking a vehicle on the road.

It must be remembered as well that apart from those accidents brought about by human factors, such as error of judgement or carelessness, the contribution made by changes in the physical environment of road and vehicle is by no means negligible.

In a paper on 'Road Safety and the Practical Use of Projective Personality Tests as Accident Predictors', the manager of The Industrial Psychological Services, Johannesburg, Mrs Lynette Shaw (1965) says: 'There is more to accident liability than frequency of involvement; there is the question of the really serious accidents. This study (i.e. the practical use of projective personality tests as accident predictors) has shown that, although because of his driving skill, a person may not be involved in many minor accidents, he can, because of personality factors, still be a dangerous risk with regard to serious speeding accidents. Such a person would probably be described as "accident-prone" by psychologists but not by statisticians. . . .' Instead, Mrs Shaw suggests the use of such terms as 'accident repeater' or 'chronic accident risk'. For the purpose of this study, therefore, the term 'accident-prone' is used in a very limited sense, which will be explained in later pages.

As suggested above, the task of studying the behaviour of motorists with a view to establishing certain behaviour patterns or personality 'traits' adverse to safe driving is, at least, difficult. The numerous variables involved, and the impossibility of controlling these variables, make the problem even more difficult of solution.

If the attempt is made to isolate just one or two factors the end result may prove or disprove the bearing or influence of these factors *only* on general motoring behaviour, while only loosely relating them in any way to the whole driving situation. At the other extreme, if it is intended to undertake a comprehensive investigation and to analyse as many factors as possible, the time involved would of necessity have to be endless and the funds available inexhaustible. Even then, there would be no certainty that, pound for pound, the end result would justify the expense of the study undertaken.

This programme of work, similar to other individual attempts at research in the various fields run on shoestring budgets, suffered acutely both from lack of funds and, as an indirect consequence, from a lack of time in which to pursue some of the many interesting features that emerged and that warranted further and detailed investigation.

Anyone who has had to undertake an individual research project knows that the consequence of these setbacks is twofold. Apart from having a depressing and frustrating influence on the worker, they have the effect of stinting some areas of study and thus quite frequently of forcing interesting and relevant data either to be left totally unexplored or to be touched upon very briefly. Owing to the pressure of time, therefore, and the necessity of working within a very limited budget, it was not possible to diversify into areas of behaviour other than some 'aggressive' and 'anxiety' traits.

The whole programme of work in relation to these two factors can, and should, be regarded as no more than a mere pilot study. Thus, in keeping within the limited use of pilot studies, it intended to attempt, if possible:

(*i*) To establish certain behaviour 'trends' within the context of aggression and anxiety in the motoring situation.

(*ii*) To bring to light any data interesting enough to warrant a full-scale, detailed, and systematic study by those financially or otherwise better equipped – hopefully, with a view to making motoring a less hazardous occupation than it has become.

The present writer feels that one or two 'findings' that have emerged do indeed warrant further investigation. If this 'scratching at the surface', as it were, succeeds in helping towards the elimination, or at least towards the control, of certain adverse factors in motoring, these efforts will have been worth while.

From author to reader

In order to present results of the following investigation in as interesting a manner as possible, the book is divided into two parts, in the effort to keep the more qualitative data separate from quantitative analysis.

Part I deals mainly with the qualitative aspects of the study, verbatim reports of interviews with motorists, and so on. This section is designed for those readers who find little or no interest in quantitative data and the mathematical presentation of statistical analysis. These have been left for discussion in the latter half of the book.

Part II is mainly concerned with areas of statistical information, sampling methods, scoring, evaluation of data, etc., and is directed mainly to persons familiar with, and interested in, the less 'narrative' areas – namely, figures and tables, correlations and frequencies.

However, owing to the importance of driving behaviour and its effect on our everyday life, whether one is a motorist or not, mathematically inclined or otherwise, all information obtained during the course of this study is, it is hoped, presented in a manner likely to be of interest to both lay and professional people.

Descriptive

PART I

Descriptive

1 Introduction and orientation

In the year to the end of 1963, in London alone, 98,503 vehicles were officially known to have been involved in some form of accident (HMSO, 1965a). Of this figure, 47,115 of the total (or 47·8%) were motor-cars or cabs; an increase of 13·5% against the figures of 1962. Nationally, road casualties numbered:

> 341,696 in 1962
> 356,179 in 1963
> 385,499 in 1964

or an average yearly increase of approximately 22,400 casualties (HMSO, 1965b). The average yearly figure for deaths as a result of road accidents was by 1963 in the region of 7,184.

Some may attempt to explain away this alarming trend by pointing to the increase in the number of motor vehicles on the roads every year – ten million plus in 1962, eleven million plus in 1963, and twelve million plus in 1964 (British Road Federation, 1964).

Yearly increases in the number of vehicles on the roads may perhaps affect the statistical probability of higher accident figures and thus constitute one of the reasons for the upward trend in accidents and their consequences. However true in theory this may be, it could certainly not be advanced as the main cause – not until it has been proved; and so far no investigation, statistical or otherwise, has conclusively made a finding based on this hypothesis. Equally, the increased number of driving-licence holders may be advanced as the chief factor in the steady rise in accident figures, although it is more plausible to suggest that the increase in the number of potentially dangerous drivers could be directly responsible for the increase in the number of road casualties.

In other words, an increase in the number of vehicles on the roads is proportional to the greater number of licence holders incorporating the 'dangerous' ones, and in turn is consequently proportional to the higher yearly accident figures.

It is not just the fact that more and more people are being granted driving licences that causes alarm, but the evidence that, in addition to the many already in possession of a licence, are those drivers who, though having successfully passed the prescribed Ministry of Transport Driving Test, are yet unfit to drive a motor vehicle. This unfitness is due to factors other than those covered by the driving-test situation, i.e. the not-so-obvious factors of adverse personality patterns or behaviour characteristics.

So far, at the official level, there is little awareness that this may be so, and solutions to the problems of accident prevention are sought elsewhere, despite questions in Parliament regarding the inadequacy of the driving test as it exists.

It may be accepted that some accidents are precipitated by 'chance situations' difficult even for the most experienced motorist to foresee. In such a context the term 'accident' carries the proper and accurate meaning. However, it would be totally incorrect to suggest (as some do) that all accidents are the result of chance situations, fate, or some such random occurrence, and therefore are bound to happen.

Many of these 'accidents' could be prevented but for the frame of mind or the personality of those involved in them – some individual quirk or attitude that sooner or later manifests itself in the kind of driving that can end in an accident. In such cases perhaps the use of the term 'involvement' instead of 'accident' would be more specific. These quirks or adverse personality characteristics are as numerous as are motorists themselves.

Broadly speaking though (if one were forming an hypothesis), they could be listed under specific headings, such as negligence, aggression, anxiety, and failure of concentration. Also high on any list of characteristics are lack of confidence and, apparently one of the most important, lack of concern for others or for self. Each could in turn be an independent attribute or the result of one of the others mentioned.

Some of these could be further sub-divided. For example, 'aggression' may be distinguished as either latent or overt, and in turn could take various forms: a driver swearing at another when thwarted, as opposed to one driving his vehicle straight at another for perhaps the same reason. One is an infinitely more dangerous act than the other.

It has already been suggested that 'consideration' in motoring is an important attribute in relation to safety. Either a driver is usually considerate or he is not. If he is not, no amount of propaganda alone will change his attitude, no legal steps can be taken to ensure that he becomes so. No one can be brought before the bench on a charge of 'bloody-mindedness' only! Yet, it would seem that some of these very attitudes to other motorists manifest themselves in the driving situation in a manner tending towards the high probability of the occurrence of an 'accident'. In short, consideration for others is like giving to a charity: you do so if you feel inclined; if you do not, well, it is entirely up to the individual.

In spite of its loose meaning, for the reader's convenience the term 'accident' will continue to be used to indicate motor-vehicle involvement in which damage to vehicle and/or injury to persons is sustained, regardless of cause.

More and more people are being made aware of the 'human' element in motoring. The following passage is quoted from a chapter on 'Personality and Driving' in a recent publication on motoring (Claridge, 1965). 'The increasing stress involved in motoring nowadays makes the psychological efficiency of the driver a more important factor than the mechanical efficiency of the vehicle he drives.'

As the introductory figures indicate, the yearly rise in the number of accidents, and the consequent increase in the number of road casualties, is alarming. Every year during the seasonal statutory holidays the public is made aware of this.

What *is* truly alarming is that too few people seriously appear even to take note of this state of affairs. Television, radio, and press reporting of the number of deaths due to road accidents during the holidays, against the previous year's figures, have become part of the holiday programme. Newscasters routinely report that only 'twenty-two people were killed on the first day . . . this is six less than on the same day last year'!

The fact that one or two hundred people have been involved in accidents, many of them fatal, seems to make little or no impression on the population, least of all on motorists themselves. What little interest is shown is usually in the nature of a pseudo-philosophical discussion, and all is forgotten until the next holiday.

The belief that 'it could never happen to me' is very strong. Almost 70% of the 382 motorists who took part in the survey professed to this belief in some sense or other. What is almost always overlooked, and what most people fail to realize, is that while they have in fact managed to avoid having serious accidents, many were probably instrumental in someone else being involved in one, sometimes deliberately, as will be shown in later pages, but more often than not because of carelessness, an apathetic approach to motoring, or other forms of accident-precipitating behaviour. Behaviour not generally tolerated in everyday life is accepted unquestioningly as being a part of motoring.

It has been suggested (Tillman & Hobbs, 1949) that 'One drives as one lives'. Lynette Shaw, in her work on personality tests as accident predictors (Shaw, 1965), further qualifies this hypothesis by suggesting that as driving offers opportunities for delusions of grandeur and anti-social behaviour, many accidents are caused by the fact that people also 'drive as they would like to live'.

Indications suggest that this is by far the more accurate of the above two statements when referring to motoring and accidents in general. In this survey, at any rate, many drivers admitted to undergoing a change in attitude when behind the wheel of a car. Some changes are for the good, but these are rare. By and large, most people take on a more aggressive nature without due regard to other road-users. Typical of the latter kind of change, a young bank clerk in his mid-twenties confessed to getting a thrill in pretending that the North Circular Road in London was a motor-racing circuit and in driving on it as though in a motor race. He would, he confessed, never afford to become a racing driver, so this was the next best thing!

The numerous penalties for speeding, dangerous driving, and the one occasion when his licence was suspended for six months after he had lost control of his car and knocked down a cyclist were all something to talk about in terms of a big joke. This young man, when interviewed in the sitting-room of his own home, appeared to be a reasonable, intelligent, sensitive type of person who, among other things, felt quite strongly against the misuse of atomic energy and the need for a greater measure of discipline for today's youth. Yet he regarded his own irresponsible behaviour on the road very lightly.

This kind of change is by no means the odd exception. Rather, it seems that people who would be willing to support charities, scorn the growth of social violence, uphold the law in other respects, and generally try to live as good citizens, change into selfish, aggressive, and dangerous beings in the time it takes to get into and start a car.

One may ask what makes an apparently perfectly normal, mild-mannered individual turn into an anti-social road maniac. The answers to such questions could be misleading in their simplicity. Theories suggest that people are subject to greater stress when driving, and the accepted belief is that under stress they tend to behave oddly. Because people are different, some types of 'personality' are more prone under such conditions to give way to their emotions, and this frequently results in the behaviour described above. Another theory is that certain individuals have what is popularly referred to as 'a power complex', and when driving, utilize the power of the vehicle as an extension of themselves. If an individual lacks 'personal drive' or dominance, either is easily afforded in the driving situation, and in compensating for this lack, he frequently over-compensates.

With regard to safety, it appears that the general attitude of 'I'm all right, Jack!' is prevalent among motorists. This illusion of safety inside a car seems to tie in with the attitude, 'It can never happen to me.' Furthermore, certain individuals and groups of motorists are unresponsive to the appeal to reason.

Researches into the various aspects of behaviour in the motoring situation have uncovered some interesting data, but until now very little has been done to make use of the findings, and the number of road casualties and deaths is, as ever, on the increase.

One is prompted to inquire whether it can be that we are past caring one way or another what is done about such a state of affairs – or can it simply be that we are not aware of its existence?

Culpin (1937) suggested that a generation has grown up side by side with a developing mechanical capacity for speed. Speed itself is not without certain advantages, but in the wrong hands can be truly lethal. Is it possible that halfway through the 'sixties a generation is growing up side by side with a developing *emotional* capacity for the thrills and dangers of speed? It would certainly appear so.

What can prevent this and similar attitudes from becoming a way of life when apparently all other attempts are failing?

National Road Safety campaigns pointing to the need for better and safer motoring, gruesome pictures in the press emphasizing certain aspects of this need, and other private attempts are felt to be over-dramatizing the situation. One concludes that the ordinary man has become hardened to this kind of approach. He considers that appeals, like the reports of road casualty figures, are only a seasonal phenomenon, and he continues with his motoring undisturbed by the 'do-gooders'!

Most people now agree that in the wrong hands the motor-car becomes a deadly weapon capable of doing much harm, apart from giving rise to certain economic and social problems. But as I have suggested earlier, many motorists unfit for the responsibility are permitted to drive. It may be after months, and often too late, that such a person is found out and stopped by law. Repeatedly we are told that the need to do something about this state of affairs has never been greater.

In a democratic country, however, extreme care is necessary in the choice of the methods employed to isolate the potentially 'unfit'; but even before legislation is framed, some effective method of assessment is desirable. Liberty is viewed as of far greater importance than life itself, and a loss of individual liberty, however small, even for the purpose of safeguarding life, would doubtless be strongly opposed.

This is a problem for the politicians and the legislators; one that will have to be faced urgently if something constructive is to be done towards making the roads safer.

The task of this study, as indicated in the preface, was to uncover imformation and attitudes regarding 'aggression' and 'anxiety' in motorists and to elicit what bearing, if any, these two factors may have on dangerous driving and on 'accident-proneness'.

For the purposes of this study, the term 'accident-prone' is applicable mainly to groups and not to individuals within a group. For instance, if a person is said to belong to an 'accident-prone' group this would merely indicate that the accident point-per-person in that group is above the average for all groups within the sample. However, individuals who contribute accident scores will be referred to as either High or Low contributors (to their group total) and symbolically represented as HC or LC (see Hypothesis, page 12).

In other parts of the world certain steps are being taken against the 'unfit' driver. These may take the form of 'driver-clinics' or schools for accident-prone drivers, set up for a specific purpose.

In such places 'accident-repeaters' are given comprehensive training to reach a standard of motoring comparable to that expected by the Institute of Advanced Motorists in Britain. Only after satisfying this standard by test are their driving licences re-issued. Some success has been achieved. For example, in a recent pilot study in Wisconsin, USA, 233 motorists with particularly bad accident records were chosen to participate in a programme of re-training. Each was interviewed, given expert advice, and subsequently re-tested. Before the consultation, the average for the group totalled 862 accidents a year. The next year the figure dropped quite dramatically, to 35 (*World Road News*, 1966a). In Chicago, USA, people frequently involved in accidents or traffic violations are given thorough psychological screenings and re-training in driving before being allowed on the roads again. Here, too, a measure of success has been reported.

In France, in an attempt to make motoring safer, new laws are being introduced with respect to speed limits for young drivers (officially recognized as the potential 'accident-precipitators'). Those under 20 years of age, and all drivers who have held a licence for less than a year, are expected to conform to a speed limit of 90 kph (56 mph). Special stickers must be affixed to the windscreen of vehicles driven by persons in these particular categories in order to ensure easy identification by the police. Additionally, in an effort to combat bad driving, roadside courts have been set up with effective powers to penalize offenders. In Britain the nearest approach has been legislation involving a motorist's disqualification after the commission of three offences. Similar immediate solutions to the motoring problem are being attempted in various parts of the world, but if any long-term success is to be expected, something more will have to be done.

In spite of all these attempts at improving road safety, it appears that there is very little general improvement in the road casualty situation internationally. Would not more drastic steps have greater effect? It has been suggested that stricter enforcement of the law by the police is one way. Indeed, this could be an effective answer if the stumbling-block of ineffective legislation were to be removed. As things stand, the police are much restricted as to their powers of enforcement. For example, a motorist may be stopped by the police for speeding or dangerous driving. The time lag between this police action and the offender's appearance in court could be anything up to six months.

Even if he happens to be a particularly or persistently dangerous driver, for six months, until his appearance in court, he is generally legally permitted to continue to drive. Even if he happens to inflict fatal injury upon someone during this period, until his case is actually heard, often weeks later, he is at liberty to continue to use his vehicle.

One solution to this problem would be to empower the police to hold driving licences until the hearing in court, as is done in France. In spite of its potential as a certain deterrent, however, this method may be open to abuse unless, in addition, there is some safeguard against exploitation or victimization. One other way of improving the situation would be to cut through the legal tangle – though such a thing may appear impossible in Britain – so that cases are heard shortly after the commission of the alleged offence and, when appropriate, licences are withdrawn.

However, these measures are all cures after the event rather than prevention before it. The only really effective way of ensuring greater safety on the roads is to reduce the number of *potentially* dangerous drivers on them.

Many large transport organizations in the United States and in some parts of Europe subject their drivers to a series of tests, in which are included batteries of psychological tests (see Review of Past Work, page 61). The results in weeding out undesirable drivers have been very encouraging. It seems plausible to suggest that such methods should be used as the official yardstick for testing the capacity of all motorists, internationally.

Economic, moral, or legal problems will surely arise, but no expense would be as great as the measurable cost of accidents in Britain, which has already reached somewhere in the region of £160–£170 million per annum. The legal and moral problems would doubtless be the greater, but these would in time, it is hoped, become insignificant by comparison with a progressively downward trend in the yearly accident figures. This, though, is a question of values.

It is widely accepted that the present means of testing drivers, the prescribed Ministry of Transport driving test, is inadequate. Even some of those carrying out the Test are not satisfied with its effectiveness in seeking out potential accident-precipitators.

In an interview with two M.O.T. driving examiners the views expressed fully upheld this belief. Others with similar attitudes included police inspectors and officers of the Traffic Division, driving instructors, insurance men, and more than 80% of those taking part in the survey.

A frequent response among the latter was, 'I wasn't really fit to drive until some months after [the Test].' Here 'fitness' was mainly related to driving 'experience', but many remain unfit even after acquiring much driving experience.

Let us turn to the M.O.T. Test and consider what it measures. Simply, it measures one's ability to perform certain basic driving tasks as follows:

A learner-driver –

1. Is tested for approximately twenty minutes only, in the weather conditions prevailing at the time of the test.

2. Is required to drive only in daylight.

3. Is asked a few questions about the Highway Code (a degree of luck is involved in being asked only the questions to which answers are known).

4. Is asked whether he is prone to certain illnesses (no documentary proof is required).

5. Is subjected to a haphazard, primitive form of eye-test.

It appears to be thought unnecessary to test a driver's knowledge of even the most basic aspects of the car engine or his ability (or inability) to drive at night, or to ascertain whether he can control the skidding of his vehicle, or whether psychologically he is fit to be in control of that vehicle under normal road conditions and so on.

Obviously no test can be made perfect, and the economic considerations have to be taken into account as well. However, tests need not be carried out entirely at the one time or by only one person. In fact, the subjective element in the test situation as it exists is what should be guarded against.

A motorist would be better tested, and with a greater degree of fairness, if at least two examinations were made at an interval of, say, two weeks or a month. Testing would be carried out by a different examiner on each occasion and a consensus of opinions or assessments accepted. This should cover only the 'mechanics' of driving, i.e. the ability to make proper use of the controls, etc.

The other aspects of the Test should require that a motorist produce a medical certificate attesting the satisfactory fulfilment of those conditions now being accepted verbally, and finally an assessment of personality by a psychologist or someone specially trained for this work. Accidents would still occur, but it may be presumed that those resulting from certain 'human' weaknesses would be greatly reduced.

No statistics are available, but from work carried out in this study there is a strong indication that the age-groups of drivers passed most often at the first attempt in the M.O.T. Test are the youngest, i.e. the 17–35-year-olds. As will be shown later, this is the most aggressive group and the one with the highest accident figures. If such is the case, there is something radically wrong with the driving test.

Ability to control a vehicle would certainly not appear to be the most important variable, and this in fact is mainly what is being assessed in present driving tests, and not very thoroughly at that! Indeed, one cannot help but quote again that 'The increasing stress involved in motoring nowadays makes the psychological efficiency of the driver a more important factor in road safety than the mechanical efficiency of the vehicle he drives . . .' and, if one is permitted further to qualify these words, '. . . or of his physical ability to control that vehicle'.

2 Hypothesis and questionnaire

In Part II of the book the lay reader will find certain references made to the effect that, so far, no *single* attribute investigated by observers in the past is valuable on its own as a predictor of accident-proneness. Rather, there is a strong indication suggesting that results have been more favourable when using a 'battery' of tests.

Therefore, one may ask why, in view of the fact that such slight value can be attached to studies of single attributes, this study should have been based on the factors of Aggression and Anxiety only. It has already been stated why the choice was made, and the reader is asked to bear in mind the nature of this study and its effectiveness in only 'feeling out' certain areas of behaviour. Earlier, emphasis was laid on the fact that it can be regarded as no more than a contribution to other more detailed studies of common behaviour patterns among motorists.

The hypothesis was formulated as follows:

(*i*) drivers displaying aggressive behaviour while driving are, as a result, more liable to have accidents;

(*ii*) drivers in a state of anxiety are, as a result, more liable to have accidents;

(*iii*) that anxiety to some extent precipitates aggressive behaviour, and vice versa;

(*iv*) certain combinations of aggression and anxiety are dangerous in motoring;

(*v*) within age-groups, the social status (i.e. marital, socio-economic, etc.) of a driver has an influence on his 'accident' contribution (high or low) to that group (see page 8);

(*vi*) certain anti-social attitudes manifest themselves in such a way as to make a person's driving dangerous;

(*vii*) skill and acuteness are not in themselves indicators of good or safe driving;

(*viii*) drivers with greater knowledge of the 'mechanics' of their vehicles are, as a result, safer motorists and use greater caution while driving;

(*ix*) certain drivers make use of their vehicles to compensate for, or to express, their psychological and physiological deficiencies.

In Part II (see page 69) we shall deal in detail with statistical results of the two preliminary studies. At this stage let it suffice to say that co-operation from those motorists approached to take part in the investigation was very encouraging. They were asked to assist in making up a list of aggressive and anxious behaviour patterns and attitudes to be vetted by experts and subsequently used as the basis for eliciting attitudes from the main study sample of motorists. The end product was the questionnaire, which was distributed by the writer, and which is explained in detail below.

THE QUESTIONNAIRE

For purposes of eliciting information from drivers about their attitudes to motoring in general, and to other road-users in particular, the only effective method was the time-honoured use of questionnaires.

With virtually no alternative as efficient, the advantage of reverting to the use of questionnaires was apparent, so let us be clear about their uses and certain of their drawbacks.

The main disadvantage in the use of questionnaires in a field of study such as undertaken here is one of subjectivity. The investigator is obliged to accept as relevant data the response given to any specific question. Occasionally, the response to a particular question may be true at the time of completion of the questionnaire but totally incorrect, or even contradictory, some days later.

If a questionnaire is designed to allow a subject to explain his responses often this method gives rise to ambiguity, apart from increasing the complexity of analysis at later stages of the study. In fact, a questionnaire is no substitute for categorized factual information (date of birth, marriage, illnesses, etc.) when details are available from other sources. However, most survey questionnaires require additional information which cannot be obtained in this way and which has to be gleaned from the subject himself. For instance, in a study concerning 'attitudes' there is no place, no official agency or government office, from which can be found out a particular person's attitude to, say, female drivers! In such a case, therefore, the only way to establish the information is to ask the person himself – either orally or by inviting him to record his attitude against a specific question on female drivers.

In this method the response given is taken at its face value, for there

C

is no practical, valid, or economical method of establishing whether or not the man *really* hates women drivers just because he says so. With few exceptions, the investigator accepts what is being admitted by the respondent.

Some questionnaires are so designed as to try to overcome this problem. They allow a subject to be more specific by giving him a range of alternatives. The most common of these is in the form of Semantic Differential rating scales. For example:

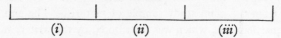

where space (*i*) represents hating women drivers,
       space (*ii*) represents indifference to them,
       space (*iii*) represents liking them.

or alternatively, depending on the investigator's choice of wording,

       space (*i*) hating them a great deal,
       space (*ii*) only slightly,
       space (*iii*) not at all.

The person completing the questionnaire is required to choose and tick only *one* space.

However, in spite of wide usage, there is still some doubt whether in fact the Semantic Differential is understood by a sufficient number of people for it to be effective for purposes of analysis.

The ideal would be an interview and a personal discussion of their attitudes with all those taking part in such a survey, but, because numbers are usually in the region of several hundred or more, considerations of cost, time, and so on have to be taken into account. Questionnaires then become obligatory, as the only other feasible method when the numbers of participants in a survey are great and time is limited. However, a useful compromise, followed in this study, is to interview a few people after they have responded to a questionnaire.

In designing the questionnaire, it is usual to be guided by a set of rules:

(*i*) that the questions asked should be explicit and should not give rise to any ambiguity or misunderstanding of how the respondent is required to interpret them;

(*ii*) that instructions should be precise, and the whole schedule designed in such a manner as to obtain maximum information.

Both these are extremely important factors.

In addition, there has been much controversy on the desired length of the questionnaire; if it is too long people tire; if too short not enough information is obtained. The length of the questionnaire, though important, is, however, only a minor problem so long as its content can be made sufficiently interesting to establish full co-operation from those who have to answer the questions.

Sometimes, as in this study, items in a questionnaire have to be 'loaded' in order to indicate certain characteristics of the person completing the questionnaire. Critics and pundits are quick to point out that in no circumstances should questions or items be 'loaded'. Very occasionally, though, this method helps, even if it is theoretically incorrect and goes against accepted standards.

When using the method of a 'one alternative choice' questionnaire, as in this investigation, where the subject must select only one of two items given, he is at a disadvantage when confronted with a desire to respond with a view that lies somewhere between the two extremes provided. For instance, when confronted with two items such as:

> *I like driving fast*   *I do not like driving fast*

and the subject is required to choose only one of these statements, if he likes driving fast on certain occasions (on the motorways, for instance) and not on others there is no provision in the items for him to say so.

In defence though, the very nature of the 'one alternative choice' questionnaire is *not* to allow the subject to use the mid-point as afforded in the rated-scaled type of questionnaire (the Semantic Differential scale, for instance) but to make him decide which of the two items is *nearer the truth for him*, however slight an edge it has over the other. Herein lies the crux of the matter. It is the indication in favour of one or the other extreme that is the criterion – not absolute accuracy.

The results of the preliminary (pilot) study made it apparent that this method would be sufficiently effective to be used for the main-study investigation.

While consideration was given to the use of scaled ratings (five-point scale), it was soon apparent that it would be virtually impossible effectively to scale all the items being used in the questionnaire. Especially was this so if its presentation to the respondent was to make some sense and to avoid complexity. For example, items (alternatives) such as:

> *I have been in a fight with another driver,*

as against

I have never been in a fight with another driver,

would be quite meaningless if a mid-point were included as an alternative to choose from. So, too, would the alternatives:

I have given chase to a driver who has annoyed me,

as against

I have never given chase to a driver who has annoyed me,

or

I have driven at another vehicle in anger,

as against

I have never driven at another vehicle in anger.

What would a mid-point indicate here?

The obvious choice is either of the two alternatives given, whichever is applicable.

Some will postulate that a way around this problem would have been not to have 'loaded' the items in the first place, but to have allowed the subject to respond in his own way, something like:

What happens when another motorist annoys you? . . .

It is fair to assume that the answer to this type of question could be more comprehensive or informative, but by the same token, it would also furnish greater room for irrelevant anecdotal material or such negative responses as:

It depends on which way he annoys me. . . .

Categorization and analysis would, as a result, be made quite difficult in the face of the 'subjectivity' of the researcher deciding which statement goes where!

Another method, the 'sentence completion' response, though useful in limited studies (see page 23, Re-rating of motorists prior to interview), employed at the above stage of the investigation would be no more effective than the use of questions like that illustrated. The same difficulties would prevail.

Additional considerations as to why the 'one alternative choice' method was adopted for use in this study were:

(*i*) easier computation – as 'trends' only were being investigated, the time that would have been required for comprehensive probing of respondents was better utilized toward s more relevant work;

(*ii*) the questionnaire was less awesome in appearance (an important point to the respondent);

(*iii*) less instruction (and consequently less room for misunder-standing by the not so intelligent) was necessary;

(*iv*) again, as 'trends' only were being investigated, 'Extreme' rating of Aggression (AG) and Anxiety (AN) was made easier;

(*v*) perhaps the most important of all, it would not have been possible comprehensibly to scale many of the items/alternatives used in the questionnaire.

PRE-SAMPLING (TIME AND PLACE OF STUDY)

The choice of area from which the sample would be drawn was more or less limited by the two factors of finance and convenience. Consequently, it became necessary for the survey to be carried out locally, and the writer's own borough, Hornsey, in London, was chosen as the most convenient area.

However, owing to the varied methods of sampling finally decided upon, a small percentage of motorists who took part in the survey were from outside the borough.

Initially, an attempt was made to draw up a list of a 'representative' sample of motorists in the borough, but this was given up in the first stages, as certain problems presented themselves.

To begin with, a list of all currently registered motorists, the raw material for sampling purposes of this kind, is held by the Licensing Authorities and is inaccessible to people other than the police. Never-theless, this in itself was no great problem. The fact was that even if such a list were made available, with allowances for the so-called 'float-ing' population, the definition of the term, 'representative' sample of motorists, would have remained, and still remains, a great problem.

It must be assumed that this is a meaningless term when applied in a general sense to the motoring population. If the sample of motorists is to be representative of the influences of social structures, then a 'repre-sentative' sample of British drivers (if an international comparison is being made) is perhaps possible. So, too, is a 'representative' sample of American motorists, or French motorists, or motorists from any other country.

In such cases it could be assumed that as there is a national (social) difference in the background of motorists drawn from these countries, these differences could have a direct bearing on the difference in driving behaviour between the national groups. But if the term 'representative' was applied to a sample of motorists from Hornsey in London this almost certainly would not effectively indicate that the 'driving' in

Hornsey is different (owing to varied social structure) from, say, a group of motorists from Morningside in Edinburgh.

Any assumption would have to be of an extremely tentative kind. This is because the roads in the country are common to all. So, too, are the traffic regulations and penalties applied to motoring offences. If differences do exist, they could plausibly be attributed to individual personality characteristics rather than to different social structures.

It can also be assumed that the 'kind' of driving experience of motorists (and consequently their driving behaviour) in Britain differs in respect to urban and rural motoring, but in order to make practical use of this hypothesis for any investigations, it would first become necessary to establish that there is in fact a different psychological influence on motorists in urban and rural areas – an interesting subject for study, but one which would require a more detailed effort than can be afforded within the scope of the work undertaken here.

Secondly, it was decided that a sample of motorists could be drawn from the electoral register. Again, this method was discarded, because it imposed two limits. All names in the register are of voters of 21 years and over; thus motorists from the 17–21 age-group – a very large number indeed – would be excluded from the sample. Also, it was found that only a minority of registered voters held driving licences, and this would have considerably reduced the potential success rate. In view of this, the problem of obtaining a sample of motorists would have been made possible only by the greater problem of increasing the number of names taken from the register in order to arrive at a working figure of about 300.

The sample was finally taken in three ways, not so much to overcome any bias that could have intruded if only one method of selection were to have been adopted, but mostly for convenience in setting up a working list of those motorists to be included in the survey within the limited time available. Briefly, for this is dealt with in greater detail later, the sample was drawn up: (*a*) by stopping every tenth vehicle at a chosen spot and approaching the driver; (*b*) by calling on registered voters who were motorists; and (*c*) by motorists volunteering to complete questionnaires. As a result, as already stated, it became necessary to include a small percentage of motorists from outside the Hornsey area.

An interesting observation made later in the analytical stage of the study showed there was very little difference between the three sample groups in their frequency of response to the questionnaire items (see Chapter 6, Samples and Sampling Methods).

It may be assumed, then, that generally speaking, motorists have similar approaches to driving, regardless of differences in social backgrounds or varied geographical locations (in this sample admittedly within a city only). However, this could perhaps add a further degree of plausibility to the assumption that there is no such thing as a 'representative' sample of motorists, using the term to describe motorists from various parts of the country.

SOME INFORMATION FROM QUESTIONNAIRE RESPONSES

Of the questionnaires received, 382 were finally used for investigation. These were responses of 279 male and 103 female motorists, ranging in age from 17 years to 70 plus.

Each response was carefully checked, coded, scored, categorized as being more or less aggressive, more or less anxious, and so on. Subsequently the results were grouped to see if any significant pattern of behaviour (i.e. professed aggression/anxiety by a respondent's choice of questionnaire items) emerged to be identified with particular age-groups.

Screening the data obtained revealed a very definite and significant pattern of both aggression and anxiety. The most obvious information was that motorists between the ages of 17 and 35, mainly male, were not only the most aggressive but also the most likely to be involved in a motor accident.

Further, it emerged that the more overt aggressive behaviour, such as *chasing another vehicle when annoyed, driving straight at another vehicle in anger, deliberately trying to edge another car off the road, fighting with other drivers*, and *difficulty in controlling one's temper when driving*, was, in the main, characteristics of the really aggressive motorist, usually to be found within the age-group 17–35.

Shortly we will look at the results of interviews carried out with the more aggressive motorists and compare them with the data from questionnaires. Here, let us continue to consider some other interesting information gleaned in this way. Aggressive tendencies in both men and women tend to diminish with age, so that by the time middle age is reached emotions are well on the way to being controlled. Anxiety feelings, on the other hand, tend with advancing age to increase among female motorists and decrease among male motorists.

This is an interesting feature that warrants further investigation. Why should the woman motorist become more anxious as she gets older?

If one assumes that driving 'experience' is an important factor a motorist should become *less* anxious with advancing age. Two explanations are possible – a physiological reason and/or a psychological cause. If it is true that a physiological factor makes a woman become more anxiety-prone as she gets older, why not the male?

No attempt was made to single out psychological factors, but it is more plausible to assume that the upward anxiety trend in the female driver population has a psychological basis; difference in temperament being the basic difference between men and women drivers. This hypothesis is borne out by the fact that women have on the whole a less aggressive nature both in and outside the motoring situation; and within it, as will be shown, they are far less accident-prone.

Mention has been made of the questionnaire responses that indicate a tendency for younger men, between the ages of 17 and 35 years, to be highly aggressive. It also emerged that they are the most accident-prone.

The reader will no doubt be interested to know who are the chief offenders within age groups. In Part II of the book the analysis of this is given in greater detail, but it will be useful to mention the findings here.

On the basis of statistical examination it transpired that marital status bore no significant influence on driving habits; that motorists from the lower-middle classes were significantly the most accident-prone (working-class people the least so) and that combinations of high aggression and high anxiety made for a greater degree of accident liability. Indeed, the trend of high aggression/anxiety/accident liability was not confined to males only. In summarizing the data obtained, the factor of aggression emerges as being all-important. Indeed, it is significantly apparent – and this will be emphasized further by the interview reports – that a tendency towards high aggression, whether or not in combination with high anxiety, is a fair indicator towards accident liability, giving aggression in the motoring situation a greater influence than anxiety.

3 The interview: design and administration

The main reasons for conducting interviews were the following:

(*i*) In order to get each motorist with whom an interview was carried out to qualify his/her choice of questionnaire items and explain or justify certain attitudes expressed. (No hypothesis was made, but *a priori* it was felt that motorists with comparable AG/AN scores and/ or accident scores would, in their answers, justify certain kinds of behaviour in a characteristic way, i.e. they would all give more or less the same reason for professing certain attitudes or forms of behaviour.)

(*ii*) As a result of attitudes and opinions being freely expressed, to give the writer a slightly better insight into the reasons why people think they behave as they do in a car.

(*iii*) Consequently, to advance understanding of the problems of 'stress' in the motoring situation.

(*iv*) To ascertain whether there was any compensation in the form of extreme aggression by motorists who showed apparent psychological and/or physical difficulties.

(*v*) To ascertain whether or not people with low AG/AN and accident scores were better informed about motoring (i.e. traffic regulations, what to do in certain weather conditions, etc.), and the running (i.e. the mechanics) of their own vehicles.

(*vi*) To ascertain how the design of the vehicle (i.e. layout of instruments, etc.) affected the driver's behaviour.

Finally, in an endeavour to establish basic social attitudes towards motorists, interviews were also held with members of the police (traffic and C.I.D.), with representatives of insurance companies, with driving instructors, and (after much difficulty in effecting co-operation) with two M.O.T. driving examiners. All of these were, by nature of their profession, highly qualified judges of motoring behaviour in varied circumstances.

FORMULATING THE 'SENTENCE COMPLETION' TECHNIQUE

The uses of the sentence-completion response are very limited. This is not a test but a means of establishing basic points, or areas, which an interviewer may enlarge or probe during the interview itself. In other words, it affords no more than a means of setting up one of two general areas of information for the interviewer to exploit – more simply, a starting point. It is limited, inasmuch as completion by a respondent of the same sentence some weeks later is very likely to produce a different response. For example, a subject may be asked to complete the sentence, 'When I drive alone, my driving speed . . .'.

He may complete it with the words '. . . is the same as always'. On another occasion he may use the words '. . . is within existing traffic conditions'. Both reasonable, but quite different. Such responses may be of value to the interviewer when, in a specific interview situation, *either* response may be used as a starting point from which to probe more thoroughly the subject's reason for speed change (or lack of it) when driving alone.

However, in employing the sentence-completion technique for the current study the writer not only used each response as an opening for discussion of specific factors but also as a tentative means of 're-rating' attitudes, etc., and a basis of comparison against the choice of items on the questionnaire. Simply, the latter was included so that a note could be made of whether or not the subject showed a tendency towards either Aggression or Anxiety both in his choice of questionnaire item and in the words he used to complete a sentence about that item.

Listed in Appendix IV are the sentences given for completion to each subject interviewed. The reader will notice the marked similarity of each sentence to its corresponding item in the questionnaire (see Appendix I). This was done in order that, as far as possible, responses could be made to statements having the same meaning. For example, item 3 in the questionnaire states, 'There are far too many zebra crossings on the road today . . .'. The corresponding statement in the sentence completion invites a response to, 'The number of zebra-crossings on the road are . . .', and so on.

A certain apprehension was felt that those completing sentences would remember their exact choice of item in the questionnaire and accordingly endeavour to respond in like manner. However, it became apparent after the first few interviews that, apart from having a vague recollection of the responses made in the questionnaire, none of the motorists interviewed could remember exactly their earlier responses, nor did they make any apparent conscious effort to do so. Consequently, responses to the sentence completion schedule were fairly spontaneous, and as a result afforded a better basis for comparison.

RE-RATING

Mention has already been made of the means of re-rating, i.e. comparisons were made between the choice of questionnaire item (was it Aggression or Anxiety or not?) and the sentence completion response (was it also an Aggressive response?)

The actual re-rating was made in two ways. The first was carried out immediately, where the interviewer (writer) made a note as each sentence was being discussed as to whether it showed a similar tendency to Aggression or not, so that the following discussions could, if necessary, be steered accordingly. The second re-rating was made in a more objective manner (back home after the interview) where all Aggressive or Anxious responses were given a score of 1, and compared with the raw score (1) of all Aggressive/Anxious choices on the questionnaire. This was applied only to the response to those sentences which showed (either by the words used or in the discussion which followed immediately, during the interview) an obvious tendency towards, or away from, expressed Aggression/Anxiety.

Those responses which, by the nature of the words used and by the course of the discussion, showed a neutral tendency were omitted, and their corresponding choice of questionnaire items, whether aggressive or not, was also overlooked. For example, in response to a sentence such as 'If the traffic-lights change to red as I approach them, I usually . . .' a motorist writes the word 'stop' to complete it. His questionnaire choice may have indicated he 'became annoyed', but in the interview he responds as above. No 'leading' was done in the interview, so that if the subject indicated no other attitude apart from admitting to stopping when the lights changed to red (an uninformative response with respect to Aggression and Anxiety) the item was omitted and, as with all other responses, comparisons were made on a percentage basis, i.e. only the actual number of items used from all those available.

Another important aspect of re-rating in this way was to indicate to what extent responses to the questionnaire items given by the whole sample of 382 motorists were accurate.

Of the 67 motorists isolated for interviews, 55 were interviewed (others were away on holiday or unobtainable after three attempts to make contact). Of these, 49, or 89·1%, showed the same tendency towards degrees of aggression and anxiety both in their sentence completion responses and in their choice of questionnaire items. Six showed a change in degree of aggression and anxiety.

Fifty-five, though a small number, justified the assumption that, on the whole, choices made in the questionnaire were accurately indicative of specific extremes with which a motorist identified his own behaviour or attitudes. (Those readers interested in how the interview sample was isolated should turn to Part II, page 95.)

CONDUCT OF THE INTERVIEW

(i) *Introduction*

Sixty-seven motorists were isolated for interviewing from the 382 in the sample. Fifty-five (23 low extreme, 27 high extreme, and 5 others) were obtainable and were eventually seen. Interviews were conducted informally in the subjects' own homes at times convenient to them, and arranged some days before either verbally or by letter.

Motorists who were listed for interviewing were told that it was a necessary part of the investigation that a certain number be interviewed in order to obtain a broader, more general set of opinions. No reference was made to the subject's own Aggression and Anxiety scores. When, on occasion, a motorist asked why it was necessary to interview *him* he was told that the names were randomly drawn from all 382 and that his happened to be one of them. Again, it was emphasized that his *own* opinions or attitudes were helping towards a clearer understanding of general motoring behaviour. By this manner of approach not one of the people contacted refused to co-operate.

Most interviews took place in the evenings, usually after a subject had had his meal and when there was ample time to spare. Occasionally respondents were seen at the weekend, when that was the only time available to them.

Interviews with the professionals (i.e. police officers, insurance men, etc.) were all conducted in their respective offices during working hours so that, if and when necessary, it was possible to refer to official documents, statistics, or any such information normally filed and usually near at hand.

(ii) *Method of recording*

As far as possible, discussions with subjects were left to follow a natural conversational course. However, on the subject of motoring ability or attitudes, people are notorious for relating lengthy anecdotal (and in the context of aggression and anxiety, sometimes irrelevant) experiences of their friends, acquaintances, and others, apart from their own. These are very often distorted versions with dramatic punctuations. It was therefore necessary to have at least some central path and standard frame of reference through which conversations could be steered. In so doing, the interview became partly structured, with responses (i.e. answers to specific questions and the subject's freely expressed attitudes) being categorized during the interview itself.

This categorization was carried out with the aid of pro-forma schedules, shown in (iii) below, and the recording of responses was thus made easier. For example, if in the course of discussion about 'accidents' a subject made some reference to traffic regulations or safety in vehicles this was immediately noted under its respective heading on the pro-forma. In this way not only was it possible to keep an account of specific opinions expressed but, where necessary, it made a convenient starting point for a specific area when the interview discussion came round to that particular aspect of motoring.

The use of a tape-recorder was contemplated, but initial reactions to this idea by some subjects suggested that, rather than jeopardize free responsiveness, the added measure of objectivity in the form of recorded interviews should be abandoned.

(iii) *The Pro-forma Schedule*

In this pro-forma, which was at all times in the interviewer's possession, *Section A* was used for making notes regarding the number and type of accidents, if any, in which the subject had been involved, as well as his attitudes to road accidents in general, i.e. how, in the subject's opinion, most of them were caused, who was responsible for them, etc. If it was noted that the subject had admitted in the questionnaire to having been involved in an accident, explanations, circumstances, etc., were sought and noted.

Section B in the pro-forma was used for making notes regarding any conviction (motoring) the interviewee admitted to. In the questionnaire, space was provided for indicating convictions specifically due to traffic offences such as speeding. *Section B* was used for making additional

AG/AN PROJECT

MALE/FEMALE   NAME ....
OCC.............   REF. NO..........
AB C1 C2 D+

A ACC M......   S......   VS......
TEXT:

B CONV. 1......   2......   3......   4......
TEXT:

C GATD   TEXT:

D GATVh   TEXT:

E Sug. & Mod.

   (*a*) *In vehicle*   (*b*) *In law, traffic reg., etc.*

---

notes about a subject's opinion as to which motorists were convicted most often and as to the kind of offences involved. Quite inevitably there was a considerable overlap of attitudes and opinions given in this section and in *Section E* (b), 'Attitudes to traffic regulations', discussed below.

The numbers 1, 2, 3, and 4 in *Section B* denote the questionnaire items regarding convictions, i.e., 1 speeding; 2, not being insured or taxed; 3, dangerous driving; 4, other offences.

Section C: GATD was a simple abbreviation for 'General attitudes to (other) drivers'. This section was used for noting aggressive/non-aggressive attitudes and opinions freely expressed by the subject. Particular attention was made to specific categories or groups of motorists towards which criticism was directed.

Section D: GATVh, i.e. 'General attitudes to vehicle'. Earlier, mention was made of investigation into whether or not vehicle design affected behaviour towards other motorists or the manner in which a vehicle was driven, perhaps as a result of frustration. This frustration might have been due to the gear-lever being placed in a position inconvenient for the driver to reach comfortably, too many blind spots in the vehicle for easy all-round vision, or the bad placing of instruments and gauges, and so on. This section was used to record any such attitudes or opinions.

Section E (a) was used for noting the interviewee's suggestions on safety features and modifications he would like in his own vehicle, and in addition what standard features should, in his opinion, be incorporated in all vehicles manufactured. Finally, as regards safety and comfort, his reasons for suggesting such changes, and the factors he considered to constitute the 'ideal' safe car.

Section E (b): This final section was used for recording a subject's suggestions for modification of traffic regulations, the law regarding convictions, the driving test, his opinion of the police, and his attitude towards law enforcement and safety propaganda.

Finally, any other information gleaned during the interview and not already categorized was noted on the back of the pro-forma and evaluated during the collation of data.

THE INTERVIEW PROPER

For the reader's convenience, interviews will be referred to under two headings, (*a*) Interviews with motorists and (*b*) Interviews with 'professionals' (i.e. those people whose professional activities enable them to obtain a somewhat greater insight into current motoring and driving problems).

Owing to space limitations and the very arduous task of reporting the essence of 55 interviews, information will be given under specific general headings with occasional reference to particular attitudes or opinions expressed.

However, before proceeding, the reader may be interested to know exactly how the interview was approached. Each section will therefore begin by explaining and illustrating this. In the following pages, where necessary, reference will be made to individuals thus:

Male, 38y 4m. High AG/High AN. One minor and one very serious accident. S.E.S.* C2. Occupation, clerk. Driver for 8 years.

* Socio-economic classification (derived from Registrar General's classification of occupations; see GRO, 1960).

(A) INTERVIEWS WITH MOTORISTS

Appointments were made, in most cases, a few days beforehand, though in some instances subjects were available for interviewing immediately.

An explanation was given to the subject as to why the interview was necessary, and that it would take at least an hour or an hour and a half to conduct. Once inside the subject's home, an attempt was made to establish an informal relationship. This was usually quite easy, as, with few exceptions, interviewees were delighted to be asked about their motoring opinions. Tea was usually offered to the writer, and this made for an exceptionally informal atmosphere in which to carry on discussions.

Their confidence having been gained, the interviewees were again told briefly about the investigation and the need for a better understanding of the human factor in motoring. They were then handed a 'sentence completion schedule' and requested to complete each sentence with the minimum of deliberation. As far as possible no other conversation was entered into during this stage, the writer busying himself with getting the pro-forma ready and generally making small reference notes of the subject's questionnaire-item choice and AG/AN score, etc.

When the interviewee had completed the sentences, discussion of each together with any noted change (i.e. from questionnaire choice to sentence completion) of aggression or anxiety was explained. Responses were written down by the writer under respective headings on the pro-forma schedule.

Whenever necessary, the subject was requested to elaborate on stated opinion or professed attitude and if possible to illustrate it by a verbal example.

Interviews varied in length from between one to two and a half hours, depending on the time available, the flow of conversation, and the subject's own desire either to cut short or to prolong the discussion.

Finally, a special note was made of any visible physiological and psychological difficulties in the subject (i.e. extreme agitation, stammering, nervousness, physical handicap, etc.). This was in accordance with (*ix*) of the Hypothesis (see page 13) and was merely done in order to see if there was any indication that a motorist was making use of his vehicle to express psychological and/or physiological deficiencies. In fact, very little of significance emerged to warrant further reference in following pages.

Area (1): Comparison between questionnaire item choice and sentence completion response

Mention has already been made that 49 out of the 55 motorists interviewed showed a similar trend in both choices. For example, people who on the questionnaire admitted to becoming easily provoked when driving usually completed the corresponding sentence in one of the following ways:

'For me to be provoked when driving is . . .'

(a) . . . a frequent or fairly frequent occurrence
(b) . . . not too difficult
(c) . . . usually unavoidable
(d) . . . one of my bad habits
(e) . . . not uncommon

and so on, typical examples of how the choice of questionnaire items and sentence completion response remained consistent. (The average interval between filling in a questionnaire and being interviewed was eleven weeks.)

Another example of consistency is shown below.

Questionnaire item choice: 'I get annoyed if the traffic-lights change to red as I approach them.' Sentence completion: 'If the traffic-lights change to red as I approach them, I usually . . .'

(a) . . . swear
(b) . . . stop, and fume
(c) . . . become annoyed, etc., are typical of how most subjects responded.

However, 6 of the 55 motorists interviewed changed, mostly to a lower level of aggression. Of these, two were in age-group 24 y 7 m–34 y 6 m and four were in age-group 34 y 7 m–44 y 6 m. The reasons given were that while they felt their choice of items in the questionnaire had, rightly, indicated the statement *nearest* to their own opinion, the sentence completion response allowed them to be more specific, and hence not as aggressive.

The reader will, no doubt, be interested in the kind of justification and variety of reasons given by those interviewed in reference to their attested attitudes and driving behaviour.

Repeated reference has been made to the apparent higher level of aggression within the 17–35-year-old age-groups. Let us then begin by

D

illustrating and examining some 'justifications' given by motorists from this group during discussions on their choice of questionnaire items and about their sentence completion responses. The examples will of necessity have to be limited in number, but it is hoped that they will convey the general trend. Starting with the more aggressive act of trying to 'edge another car off the road when annoyed':

Subject: Male, 28y 4m. High AG/High AN. One serious and two minor accidents. S.E.S. C1. Occupation, accountant. Driver for 6 years.

SUBJECT: . . . I have never actually edged another car right off the road but, to be perfectly honest, I have tried to on a few occasions. Why? Because I get annoyed, or to teach someone a lesson. I remember once, about six months ago, being followed by this bloke with his car headlamps fully on. I thought at first he wanted to overtake me, so I pulled over to the side to let him pass – he didn't. In fact, every time I allowed him to overtake he slowed down as I did. Eventually I became so annoyed I pulled up, thinking he would also stop. He carried on and as the car passed mine I noticed three blokes, all about twenty or so, were in it. They hooted at me, gave me the V sign and drove off. I was pretty annoyed, so I chased after them and gave them the same treatment. It developed into a running battle, and at one point I drove up alongside and gradually crowded their car into the dirt. I was so angry that I would have gone on crowding them right off if I hadn't noticed a police-car behind. It turned out that they (i.e. the police) had seen it all and we both landed up in court. I got a £15 fine for dangerous driving. I think the other bloke was also fined £15. I think I would have disqualified them from driving if I had been the judge.

INTERVIEWER: Did your own behaviour not warrant disqualification?

SUBJECT: No, I don't think so. I know my own driving could have been dangerous, but at least I was able to control my car. The other bloke was all over the place – as far as I was concerned, he deserved a good lesson and after all, he had started it!

INTERVIEWER: In similar circumstances would you do it again?

SUBJECT: I don't know – I was pretty annoyed then. I'd have to be in a real temper to do it, I suppose. I just feel there are too many yobbos around today, and someone ought to teach them a thing or two . . . Yes, I feel justified in taking the law into my own hands, the police can't be everywhere can they?

In the questionnaire this motorist admitted to losing his temper easily when driving, arguing with other drivers, using the horn a great deal, driving faster when alone, feeling impatience at traffic-lights, on occasion having felt like gladly killing another driver, and disliking drivers in certain types of cars. He justified all of these things in a very self-convincing manner. By way of illustration, consider his sentence-completion response to the opening 'To dislike drivers in certain types of cars is . . .', which was '. . . prejudice pure and simple, but extremely satisfying'.

INTERVIEWER: Whom and why?

SUBJECT: . . . It's not so much types of cars, but people who drive certain makes annoy me. For instance, I have a thing about Jaguar drivers; they are always trying to race, think they own the road. If I see one behind me, in my mirror, I go on the offensive immediately. I give them a run for their money by making sure they can't overtake so that they have to slow down to the flow of traffic instead of trying to speed all over the place. I don't like blokes in sports cars either, M.G.s and things like that. They're no better, cut in front of you without signalling. When I see one of them about I give him a warning look and if he tries messing about I hoot him like hell. . . .

INTERVIEWER: How do you mean?

SUBJECT: If he keeps cutting in I drive up close behind him and hoot . . .

The reader will, by this time, have a picture of the kind of motorist who was interviewed above. From his manner of conversation, his occupation, his home surroundings, his neat appearance, one would imagine a perfectly reasonable sort of individual. Indeed, he was extremely polite, well-spoken, and had all the outward appearance of a respectable citizen. However, from the above admissions (spoken in a very matter-of-fact way) one may see another and dangerous side. The self-appointed judge and jury of motoring behaviour; someone easily given to bad temper with the occasional dangerous associative act; someone only aware of his own behaviour as being 'perhaps' dangerous and justified by a warped sense of duty. 'Someone's got to teach them a lesson.' A direct question asking him to evaluate his own motoring behaviour elicited the following response:

'You could say I was a driver aware of the fact that some motorists are dangerous to others and aware of the need that something be done.

The only way people learn is the hard way – you've got to frighten them into changing their ways. Reasoning alone is not much use.'

Perhaps such specific idiosyncrasies are atypical, but an underlying pattern in the context of what this motorist said is common to the responses of most 16–35-year-olds interviewed, namely, 'something ought to be done about people who drive dangerously, my own aggressiveness is necessary'!

To give another example of justification by a motorist, of his own admitted aggressive behaviour – this time in reference to the questionnaire item, 'I have driven at another vehicle in anger' – consider the following illustration. The offender in this case was:

Male, 26y 6m. High AG/High AN. One serious and one very serious accident. S.E.S. C2. Occupation, shipping clerk. Driver for 7 years.

At the age of 23 years he had been disqualified from driving for two years after having knocked down a woman on a zebra crossing. The woman miraculously survived, but had broken ribs and fractured pelvis and collar bones. (This was the 'very serious' accident.)

Even at the time of interview, the subject was waiting to hear from the police about another 'serious' accident in which he had been involved some five weeks earlier – a multiple car collision on the M 1 motorway. He said, 'I had nothing to do with the cause: my car skidded and the car behind ran into me; I was pushed into a car in front. . . .'

What about his driving at another vehicle in anger, the interviewer asked.

SUBJECT: It happened some time before the first accident (the woman on the zebra crossing). I wasn't too well that day, and I hadn't wanted to go to work. But I'd only had the job for a few weeks, so I thought I'd better go in. Everything went wrong that day, I had a row with one of the other clerks about an invoice or something and then after work I found I'd been given a £2 ticket for parking my car to cause obstruction. One thing and another, the rush hour got on my nerves. Then, when I was almost home, following slowly behind a line of traffic, the car in front stopped and the chap decided to park there with a whole lot of cars behind him. I was furious and tooted him, but he waved me on, telling me to drive round his car. People (drivers) behind were also tooting, but he started walking away, so I drove my car right into the back of his. Luckily, there was no one inside his car because the boot and rear bumper were badly dented. My nearside headlamp was also smashed. The man came running back and tried to drag me out of my car, but a few other drivers from behind got out and pulled him away. There was a terrific argument then, and in the end he drove off after taking my number and all that. I never heard from him though.

INTERVIEWER: How did you feel after all this?

SUBJECT: Bloody marvellous – if I wasn't feeling so lousy that day, I would have smashed his face in too!

INTERVIEWER: Now that you look back on what happened, what is your attitude?

SUBJECT: I still think he got what he deserved – I'm sorry about my own car being smashed, but it was worth it. I mean it's blokes like him that should be picked up, the ones that cause all the trouble. I couldn't just sit there and let him get away with it, could I?

INTERVIEWER: It could have been dangerous if there were people in the back seat of his car – don't you think?

SUBJECT: Maybe, but there weren't any, and anyway, he should have thought of that. He only got what was coming.

One wonders how many people in fact follow the same line of reasoning as the motorist above when thwarted in some way? The answer to this is that there are perhaps more than is commonly believed. Admittedly, not all people go to the extreme of driving their cars into other vehicles, but other forms of expressed aggression are dangerously near this kind of behaviour.

Take, for example, this young woman (one of the very few really aggressive ones).

Female, 20y. High AG/High AN. One serious accident. S.E.S. C2. Occupation, invoice clerk. Driver for 2 years.

SUBJECT: Men think they own the roads. I always find them trying to overtake me, as though I was holding up the traffic. I've become quite fed up, and now when I notice someone trying to overtake I accelerate and don't let them pass – you should see the looks on their faces when I shoot forward – really funny.

In the course of discussion it transpired that the 'serious' accident she had admitted to was, in fact, due to someone trying to overtake her.

SUBJECT: Instead of taking the hint and knowing when he was beaten, he kept trying to overtake, hooting me all the time. Eventually, I let him pass, but when he got in front of me he braked hard. I wasn't expecting it and lost control of the car for a few seconds. I scraped a pillar-box and knocked my head against the side of the windscreen. The car swerved off the road and ended up inches away from a shop window. Luckily, there weren't many people about. I don't remember much else; I must have been knocked out almost immediately for a while, because I woke up in an ambulance on the way to hospital. I wasn't admitted though. As for the other driver, he must have driven off when he saw what happened.

INTERVIEWER: By not letting him overtake you in the first place don't you think you asked for trouble?

SUBJECT: Yes, but it's one thing to race and quite another to behave dangerously. He must have been mad or something.

A rather naïve statement, especially so from a person who admitted to disliking someone overtaking her and who confirmed her questionnaire choice by her sentence completion response:
    'When I'm being overtaken by another car I . . . accelerate.'
Interview after interview with motorists brought forth expressions of justification for aggressive behaviour similar to those illustrated above. Not one of the people interviewed in this category admitted that he was, in any way, the guilty party. Not one admitted to having learnt a lesson as a consequence of which he had made a conscious effort towards becoming a better motorist. Almost all agreed they would again do the same thing in like circumstances. Bravado perhaps, but one does not expect men of thirty or so to indulge in what is, after all, a juvenile show of strength. The following is an example of such childishness.

Subject: Male, 32y 3m. High AG/High AN. One serious accident. S.E.S. C2. Occupation, store salesman. Driver for 11 years.

Questionnaire item: 'I find it difficult to control my temper when driving.' Sentence completion response: 'Controlling my temper when driving is . . . almost impossible.'

INTERVIEWER: Why?

SUBJECT: I'm a naturally aggressive person – I mean I get into a temper easily and more so when I'm driving. You see so many b.f.s about, they're enough to annoy anyone. Old people, for instance, they shouldn't be allowed to drive, always crawling along and holding up the traffic. The young people who bring out their fancy home-made cars and try to race everyone; learner drivers – I know they've got to learn some-where, but I discourage them if I'm behind one. How? Well, if I notice he's mucking about, crawling along, I drive up right near behind him and stay on his tail for a while.

INTERVIEWER: Why?

SUBJECT: So that he will probably give up driving or get on with it the next time.

INTERVIEWER: Were you never a learner-driver yourself?

SUBJECT: Not me, mate; I learnt driving in the Forces, none of this mucking about. You know, they should only allow people who are not nervous to drive. I bet half the accidents are caused by beginners muck-ing about because they're scared stiff.

INTERVIEWER: And you feel you're helping them?

SUBJECT: Well, if it helps them to make up their minds, I am. What I do probably sounds bad, but it isn't really – it helps them to concentrate more.

A confirmed bully, this man, with a juvenile desire to play the big 'I'm not afraid' role. Getting him to talk about his own 'accident' wasn't very easy, but by playing along and humouring his opinions a rather interesting account was given.

SUBJECT: About four or five years ago I used to hire cars for the week-end. I was just out of the Forces then and would drive up to Birming-ham to see a girl. One Saturday night we'd had a lot to drink, and when I drove on to the motorway I could have sworn I was in the wrong carriageway. You know how it is at night, difficult to tell on which side the lights are? Anyway, I thought I was on the wrong side, and for once in my life I was really scared. I pulled over in a hurry a bit too quickly and drove alongside a metal fence-thing. The nearside door was scraped off and J—, my girl, was pretty cut over the arm and leg. When we stopped eventually I noticed we were on the right side after all (i.e. in the correct carriageway), and I can't tell you how relieved I was. We managed to get home eventually, but I was afraid the coppers would catch up, what with me being tight and all. . . .

INTERVIEWER: Why were you scared?

SUBJECT: Wouldn't you be if you thought you were on the wrong side of a motorway?

INTERVIEWER: Don't you think the L-drivers you spoke of earlier may also get scared by you following them as you do?

SUBJECT: Yeah, sure, but that's different, I mean that's the idea – and at least they can see me coming (he never does it at night) and besides, they have someone with them.

It was extremely difficult to follow the man's reasoning or to pinpoint his logic, but the reader will gain as much as is necessary in the illustration of yet another 'justification'.

The writer has a considerable amount of data on reasons people give for behaving as they do. The examples given are typical of this data in so far as they illustrate the varieties of justification for adverse driving behaviour, the total lack often of any understandable reasoning in the offender's logic, and the awful thought that such people with such logic are not entirely unique in among the very large motoring population – there are more by far than one imagines.

Below is yet another illustration of this strange logic and the justification of admitted aggressive behaviour as shown in both questionnaire choice and in the corresponding sentence completion response.

Subject: Male, 27y 4m. High AG/High AN. One serious, two minor accidents. S.E.S. C2. Occupation, bookmaker's assistant. Driver for 7 years.

Questionnaire item: 'If another driver makes a rude sign at me I do something about it.' Sentence completion: 'If another driver makes a rude sign at me I . . . usually chase after him and have it out.'

This motorist also admitted to having been in a fight with another driver and, as one would expect in view of the above admission, to becoming easily provoked when driving.

SUBJECT: There are two kinds of people I really hate in cars. Old women and those who use bad language or make, as you call it, rude signs. I think after the age of about 40 a woman should be banned from driving. I'm not too happy about women drivers at the best of times, but old women I just can't stand. To begin with, they are always the ones who seem to be out for a joy-ride when everyone else is in a hurry to get somewhere. Have you ever followed one? Never know what to expect next. Not a clue about traffic signalling or anything. Get them off the road, I say. As for those people who make rude signs. They're mostly punks, and they get me so riled up that I find I'm chasing them all over the place to catch up. I've had four fights altogether – once I broke a chap's nose, I think. (He sounded very proud of this.)

INTERVIEWER: Why do you do it?

SUBJECT: Because too many people are willing to let them get away with it; not me, I'm out to show them that here's one person who's not going to ignore their rudeness. It gives me a personal satisfaction to scare the pants off them when I can.

INTERVIEWER: Is it not dangerous, your chasing them about?

SUBJECT: I'm not concerned about danger, I'm usually too angry to worry about it.

INTERVIEWER: And the danger to other road users or bystanders when you drive in a state of temper?

SUBJECT: I don't give them much thought frankly, I'm usually concentrating on catching up with the car I'm chasing. Anyway, I'm in full control of my car.

This man had in the questionnaire admitted that his mood influenced his driving behaviour. In view of his comments above, he was asked to explain this.

SUBJECT: Well, I admit my driving must be a bit worse when I'm in a bad mood, but not so you would notice.

INTERVIEWER: In what way then?

SUBJECT: I suppose it makes me less aware of other traffic and sometimes more angry towards them. If I'm trying to catch up with someone and the car in front is blocking my way by moving slowly I flash my lights or use the horn or something like that – I suppose you could say I was less considerate when I'm in a bad mood, but this is only when I'm chasing another driver.

INTERVIEWER: Usually because of a rude sign? Is it necessary to retaliate?

SUBJECT: I think it is, I don't believe in turning the other cheek. I don't make rude signs myself, so the only way to pay someone back who does it to me is to knock some manners into him. I feel quite justified in doing that.

A noble gesture, but another example of how a motorist takes the law into his own hands. Such 'crusades' are hardly desirable.

Finally, before moving on to responses made in the category of the next heading, it is as well to include one more example of self-justification for aggression, one with a rather different influence, as the following account illustrates.

Subject: Male, 19 y 7 m. High AG/High AN. One very serious accident.
S.E.S. C1. Occupation, trainee manager. Driver for 2 years.

This motorist had one of the most aggressive scores in the sample, having admitted to all forms of aggressive behaviour illustrated in the examples already shown, also to having had a very serious accident. Was he an aggressive motorist?

No, he didn't think so.

How would he describe an aggressive motorist?

SUBJECT: A person who is always in trouble with the police, someone who drives flashy (i.e. expensive) cars, someone who is always having accidents.

A very peculiar interpretation indeed!

The following are some of his sentence completion responses:

'When another driver does something silly I . . . become angry.'

'For me, fighting with another driver is . . . unavoidable, because I'm quick-tempered.'

'For me to drive fast . . . is the way I always drive.'

'When I'm being overtaken by another car I . . . never let him pass if I can help it.'

'I use the horn . . . to let someone know I'm annoyed.'

'Controlling my temper when driving . . . is very difficult.'

'To dislike drivers in certain types of cars is . . . perfectly natural.'

'To take a risk when driving . . . is very exhilarating.' And so on. Unbelievable?

These were read back to him and he was asked to comment.

SUBJECT: There's nothing wrong with doing that (this was said in all seriousness). I bet most people behave like that when driving. It's perfectly natural. Why? Because everyone else drives like that. When I was taught driving (privately) my dad told me that the only way to become a good motorist was to make sure no one got the better of you.

Dangerous advice – was it true? Conveniently, 'Dad', a stockbroker, was home that evening, and confirmed this while adding some very interesting views of his own to the discussion. In fact, it was obvious that father and son were two of a kind.

This is another area for more thorough investigation; i.e. does driving behaviour run in families, and what chances are there of a young person inheriting adverse motoring attitudes from the anti-social attitudes of parents?

To return to the subject in question: What were the circumstances of his accident?

SUBJECT: Dad was driving and I was in the front with him. Mum was in the back with D— (his younger brother). We were on our way home from the West End at about six in the evening. Near Hampstead Lane a chap tried to overtake us in a Mini, flashing his lights. Dad hates Minis and refused to let him pass. Mum was shouting in the back and the Mini started to try and overtake on the inside – Dad was yelling at Mum to keep quiet so he could concentrate, and suddenly there was a terrific thump, the Mini had come too near, and somehow his bumper got caught on ours. Dad stopped, but by this time the car behind was a wreck – his whole bonnet, one wing, and the grille were smashed. I think he (the driver) was cut in the face and head – Mum almost fainted. It was quite a mess really. (All this was related amid laughter and was told with real gusto, with 'Dad' chipping in occasionally.)

INTERVIEWER: Who was to blame?

SUBJECT: Who? The Mini of course; if he hadn't flashed his lights like that Dad would have let him pass, even though he doesn't like them. . . . (His father nodded his agreement.)

There is not much one can say about the above example, it speaks for itself.

Area (2): Accidents and convictions

Some mention has been made of causes of accidents, and in one or two cases, of consequent convictions. Subjects were asked to give their opinions as to the kind of people who caused most accidents and those who were mostly convicted for motoring offences. A tall order perhaps, but one that promised some interesting responses, at the same time establishing attitudes and prejudices. Below are some typical examples of responses given by those interviewed. For the sake of brevity, only the gist of what was said is shown.

(a) ON ACCIDENTS

(i) Younger people – specifically those between 17 and 25 years – are inclined to have more accidents because they show off so much. (Man aged 49 years.)

(*ii*) Accident-prone drivers? Young drivers in sports cars. (Man aged 36 years.)

(*iii*) Mostly young people of about 20, with low intelligence. (Woman aged 24 years.)

(*iv*) People of my age. (Man aged 21 years.)

(*v*) Older people, about fiftyish. (Woman aged 58 years.)

(*vi*) Bad-tempered people, mostly young ones, 20 years or so. (Woman aged 25 years.)

(*vii*) Girls in early twenties – more nervous – and lorry drivers. (Man aged 22 years.)

(*viii*) Those between 18 and 22 years. (Man aged 35 years.)

(*ix*) Rich young people who have nothing to lose by driving carelessly. (Man aged 40 years.)

(*x*) Young drivers . . . up to 21 years or so. (Man aged 24 years.)

(*xi*) Very young and very old motorists – the young for driving to impress, the old for being physically incapable. (Man aged 33 years.)

Obviously, these are but a few opinions chosen at random, but they fairly and accurately gauge the overall impression held by the motoring population – that younger drivers *are* apt to be more accident-prone. Even though the opinions of 'professional' people are being dealt with under a separate heading, for further confirmation of the above generally accepted image of the accident-prone, it will be expedient to include one or two 'expert's' remarks here.

(*i*) Without a doubt, young men between the ages of 17 and 24–25 years. (Traffic police inspector.)

(*ii*) Men, 17–18 years to about 25 years. (Insurance man.)

(*iii*) Mostly men from 17–18 years to anywhere up to 30 years. (Driving instructor.)

(*iv*) Young lads of about twenty or so. (M.O.T. driving examiner.)

A unanimous opinion, and not without basis. With the exception of the M.O.T. examiner and driving instructors, who were administratively ill equipped, others backed up their statements with documentary proof of one kind or another.

The point here is not so much to explain why road accidents are caused but to try to show *how* some are brought about and who are mostly responsible. By their own comments, confirmed by the opinions of others and in the light of certain documentary indications, younger motorists are indeed the chief offenders. This, however, does not exclude those older motorists who, because of their exerted aggression, also identify themselves with the younger age-group in terms of accident liability. An example of this under the above heading of 'accidents' may be seen in the following account.

Subject: Male, 47y 8m. High AG/High AN. One serious accident. S.E.S. C1. Occupation, businessman. Driver for 20 years.

He believed that 'Aggressive driving is better driving'. Asked to explain:

SUBJECT: When I say aggressive driving is better driving, I mean that one ought not to be submissive when driving a car. If you wait for someone to be polite, you've got a long wait. This is a world where every man's for himself and that goes in motoring too. I never wait for people to 'wave me on' – you spend too much time waiting. I just drive on – they've got to stop, I mean no one wants to drive into you, so they stop if you're far enough out into the road, say joining the main road from a side one.

Quite a reasonable attitude some would say; but consider the man's account of his accident.

SUBJECT: I've already said I'm an aggressive person, in or out of a car – I think it's necessary to get on in life! I suppose you could say I'm a bit quick tempered too. About two years ago I went out in the morning – I drive to work daily – after having had a row with my wife. I drove pretty recklessly that day and banged the car up some.

INTERVIEWER: How?

SUBJECT: Well, it was silly, I suppose, but I couldn't be bothered waiting behind a queue of traffic, so I pulled out and overtook the cars in front. When I tried to join the line again this chap in a broken-down old thing refused to let me in – I called out angrily, but he laughed, so I eased in and edged him further away until I was fairly well in the line of traffic. He had to fall back, but kept bumping me every time the cars had to stop. This went on for quite a while, so I put my car into reverse and backed into his. That stopped him, but it ruined my rear wing and lights. I got out and took his number, etc., and threatened him with court if he didn't meet the bill . . . the fool did!

This man was very pleased with himself and his ability not only to turn the tables on his adversary but to exploit the situation as well, even though he himself had instigated it. Not such a reasonable thing to do, after all.

(b) ON CONVICTIONS

As with the above area, interviewees were asked to explain the circumstances of their motoring convictions, if any. It was quite useless to inquire about their general opinions in respect of who (i.e. which types of motorists) were most likely to be convicted, as motoring offences are numerous and one had to stipulate specific offences. In so far as speeding and dangerous driving could reasonably be incorporated into the context of aggression, motorists interviewed were asked to give their opinions of who were the chief offenders in these two categories of motoring offences. It was appreciated that the two could be analogous; nevertheless, listed below are some of the typical responses given. Again only the gist of what was said is given.

Speeding

    (*i*) . . . mostly young drivers in sports cars and Minis. (Man aged 27.)

    (*ii*) . . . young men between the ages of 17 and 25 years. (Man aged 31.)

    (*iii*) . . . young people in their early twenties. (Man aged 36.)

    (*iv*) . . . single men of 25 years or so. (Woman aged 56.)

    (*v*) . . . dare-devil young people about 20. (Man aged 48.)

Dangerous driving

Responses from the same people.

    (*i*) . . . alcoholics . . .

    (*ii*) . . . people who speed carelessly. 20-year-olds . . .

    (*iii*) . . . very young and very old people . . .

    (*iv*) . . . single men again . . .

    (*v*) . . . young people who are inconsiderate . . .

Additionally, the professionals, when asked for their opinions, were again unanimous about the young age-groups being the chief offenders.

By grouping the convictions of those people interviewed it was found that most convictions were for: (*i*) Speeding; (*ii*) Dangerous driving; (*iii*) No insurance cover or road tax; (*iv*) Others (i.e. driving under the influence of alcohol or drugs, obstruction, 'borrowing' cars, etc.).

The main incidence of Block One (i.e. High AG/High AN) motorists was in the first two groups, those of speeding and dangerous driving.

Motorists convicted for lack of insurance cover and road tax were found to include a greater number of Block Three scores (i.e. those with Low AG/High AN). However, such indications were of academic interest only and were not tested for significance owing to the small numbers available.

Area (3): Attitudes to other motorists

This area of the interview was concerned with evaluating a subject's attitude to other motorists in general and of noting specific likes or dislikes, if and when any were voiced. Quite inevitably some prejudices and attitudes have been illustrated in earlier comments, but it will do no harm to include additional information on the subject.

Interviewees were asked the question:

'What is your opinion of other motorists?'

This was general enough to get them started on any particular like or dislike or to sermonize on their pet theories or philosophies about others.

Most of those interviewed agreed that the national standard of motoring generally was rather good. Not a few compared motoring in Britain to driving in other countries and, with only rare exceptions, concluded in favour of 'home traffic'. However, certain individual opinions were characteristic of specific age groups. For instance, near enough to 80% of motorists between the ages of 18 and 30 interviewed, in one way or another accused those older of being inconsiderate.

Those 35 years and over in turn accused the younger age-groups of being reckless, immature, and incompetent, while the 30–35-year-olds, apparently in a transitional stage, blamed no one. Indeed, the differences of opinion between the younger and older motorists interviewed were very striking and typical of both sexes.

Unless by some incalculated means such differences indicated arose by chance, one assumes that up until the age of 30 a motorist identifies himself/herself with the behaviour and attitudes professed against older motorists. During the years 30–35 one is in some kind of transitional stage in which one gradually learns to control motoring belligerency, and upon reaching 35 one takes on a more sophisticated attitude of condemnation towards the younger motorist. In short, motoring attitudinal maturity follows a rather regular pattern.

There *are* individual differences which, as shown in one of the earlier examples, manifest themselves in ways identifiable with motorists of other groups but, by and large, the above pattern holds true.

Area (4): Attitudes to vehicle

In Area 4, emphasis was on a subject's attitude to his own vehicle and to his 'ideal' vehicle, and on his dislikes directed at any specific makes or type of car.

The extent of individual opinions expressed in reference to one's car is too great to enumerate here. It will suffice to illustrate some of the more common grouses against standard manufactured vehicles, as expressed by motorists interviewed.

A recurrent complaint was against the 'blind-spot' feature in vehicles. This varied with different makes, but no vehicle, in the light of discussion, was free from a blind spot. The effect on some motorists was to make them very annoyed at frequently having to contort themselves into grossly uncomfortable positions in order to have all-round vision. Mirrors placed in strategic positions eased the strain in some cases, but never completely remedied the problem.

Another common annoying feature was the positioning of control pedals too near each other. A man with large feet complained bitterly about having to live with the strain of avoiding the brake pedal when the accelerator was desired, or vice versa. In an emergency, he admitted, this could prove disastrous. In the meanwhile it was extremely nerve-racking and made him very quick-tempered.

The positioning of gauges and dials also came in for considerable criticism. 'It's very annoying,' one man said, 'being unable to read off the dials at a glance from a comfortable driving position – bloody annoying!' This statement sums up the general attitude of motorists to the layout of the instrument panels. Of significance in our present context is the bad design of vehicles that becomes an additional spur to aggression or anxiety.

Some motorists admitted to intensely 'hating' their vehicles for some fault in design. When one considers the amount of time spent in a car it is to be appreciated that man and motor should get along! Certainly this is desirable if the alternative is that a motorist takes out his prolonged anguish and anxiety on other road-users.

Still on the subject of man and car, what about those people who have a more than driving knowledge of their vehicles? The reader may recall that this was one of the areas listed for investigation.

The manner in which this was undertaken was arbitrary, but nevertheless gave a fairly clear indication. For instance, during the discussion on 'attitudes to vehicle', and the following area 'modifications to vehicles', a subjective evaluation was made of the subject's knowledge of his vehicle. The writer by no means professes to be an 'A grade' motor mechanic. On the contrary, he had much to learn from discussion with those motorists obviously knowledgeable. However, it is not a very difficult task to evaluate whether or not a person knows more or less about the workings of his car. Such was the basis for categorization and, as applicable, an appropriate note was made on the subject's pro-forma schedule to be compared with his AG/AN and accident score later.

When this was done, it was found that of those people interviewed with Low AG/Low AN (Low extreme group) or accident scores, an apparently significant number (20 out of 23) were classified as knowledgeable. On the other hand, only 8 out of 27 from the High extreme group showed any mechanical know-how. Of the five others (i.e. high accident scores but not in either extreme group), only one motorist indicated any knowledge.

The subjective basis of evaluation could, in all fairness, be questioned if one were to make any statistical inferences, but in so far as indicating that a knowledge of mechanics could be influential in accident-prevention, the above exercise is valuable, especially so when one considers that there were not a few women in the Low extreme group.

Area (5): Suggestions for safer vehicles

The next area dealt with general suggestions to the incorporation of safety devices or modification of existing features. Attitudes to safety-belts were many and diverse. Some suggestions, e.g. 'Front stop-lights', were perhaps too ambitious. Most suggestions were serious and practicable.

However, 'safety in cars' has been a major international issue recently and has received much attention in the press. Therefore it will be meaningless to reiterate the deficiencies of many vehicles manufactured, in the views of the people interviewed. Nevertheless, it is perhaps worth emphasizing that in spite of the 'false security' (mentioned on page 7), some motorists *are* in a state of acute anxiety about their personal well-being should they have the 'misfortune' to have an accident, however slight.

This much was indicated by the explanations of a few motorists, mostly female, to the questionnaire item, 'At times I have thoughts of, and picture myself in, an accident.'

To illustrate this best, we will take the sentence completion response and subsequent discussion by a woman motorist.

E

Subject: Female, 45. High AN/Low AG. No accidents. S.E.S. C1. Occupation, company secretary. Driver for 15 years.

Sentence completion: 'With me, having thoughts of, and picturing myself in, an accident is . . . a not infrequent and disturbing experience.'

SUBJECT: It's not that I lack confidence in driving – it's the fact that I lack confidence in my car. Not that it won't do a hundred miles an hour or that it's not powerful enough; these things don't bother me. What does, is the awful thought that I'm not really safe in it if I should have an accident. One hears so much about people being impaled by steering-wheels, being showered by broken glass and so on, that it makes me shudder whenever I think of it – which is very often. Quite honestly, I don't feel that cars today are strong enough to take even the slightest impact without danger to the occupants – all gilded tin, lovely to look at but quite unsafe. Structurally unsafe really. . . .

This woman was not alone in her fear of unsafe cars. Some others expressed similar anxieties.

If so small a sample of motorists includes a few like the above, one wonders how many there are in the entire motoring population with the same problem. The fact is that too much emphasis is placed on 'how fast a car can travel' instead of 'how safe it really is'. Hopefully one awaits the outcome of the present drive on safety measures in road vehicles.

The following list contains a few suggestions for safety features in all cars, noted in the course of interviews. Many have been proposed elsewhere:

1. Collapsible adjustable steering-columns.
2. Padded interiors (especially dashboards).
3. Locks or locking devices to be flush with the body of the car and to be 'child-proof' (especially in the back).
4. Stronger chassis frame.
5. Engine built on an incline so that in head-on collisions it slides under the driver's seat and not into him.
6. Rear seats facing the back (apparently there is some evidence from aeroplane crashes to suggest that people seated facing the back were the least hurt).
7. Some means of securing tip-up front seats (especially the driver's) to the floor.
8. Warning devices to call attention to faulty steering column, wheel alignment, unadjusted brakes, etc.

9. Adjustable seats to cater for different body builds.
10. Rear window de-misters and wipers.
11. Air vents.

Area (6): Attitudes to motoring law and propaganda

Finally, this area illustrates some expressed opinions of traffic regulations, of the law, etc., uses and abuses of motoring propaganda, and general evaluations of the present M.O.T. driving test.

With reference to traffic regulations and traffic law, almost unanimously those interviewed expressed concern for the gross deficiencies.

There is too much inefficiency by the police – they should uphold the law more severely, too many young hoodlums freely terrorize others and get away with it. (Male aged 52 years.)

Or alternatively: The police are inclined to nab only young people – they turn a blind eye to commercial vehicles and taxi cabs. (Male aged 24 years.)

The police in fact are overworked and far too bound by strict regulations to be really effective. Some references to this have already been made, and the matter will be discussed again a little later.

Road signs are apparently another source of frustration:

Minimize the laws – far too many signs – so that the general motorist can understand them . . .

Too complicated, considering all kinds of intelligences have to follow them . . . (Lecturer in law.)

I would like to see legislation against 'Tiger in tank' type adverts, and stricter testing regulations for vehicles. . . .

Right-of-way should be more explicit. . . .

Tests for all cars every year, and should be more thorough – including tyres, etc. . . .

Spot checks for all vehicles, even after M.O.T. vehicle test, to keep consistent standard. . . .

These are only some of the responses. Admittedly there will always be some to contradict the efficiency of any law or regulation, but some of the present traffic laws do call for substantial modification, if not a complete overhaul.

However, the point of asking interviewees to express their opinions on traffic regulations was mainly in order to establish whether or not certain regulations influenced a motorist's aggression or anxiety. Many grouses were expressed, but generally nothing of any significance was learned.

Attitudes towards propaganda, though, and the use of means of instructing the motorist about road safety produced some interesting responses.

The general feeling was that: (a) road safety 'commercials' on TV were funny but of value to school children only, and (b) road safety posters did no more than clutter up the roadside.

However, even though one would hardly be likely to accept the uselessness of road safety campaigns like those above on the strength of attitudes expressed by a relative handful of motorists, the effect of such propaganda on some road-users in terms of annoyance (and consequently aggression) is rather interesting.

It was observed, for example, that some of the motorists interviewed made rather disparaging remarks about poster slogans like 'don't drink and drive', which illustrated a gory, and no doubt intentional, emphasis on death on the roads.

The following is one such disparaging remark from a man aged 46, who had driven without accident for eighteen years. 'I'm all in favour of road safety campaigns, but I think it is absolutely disgusting putting up things like that. I feel truly nauseated and very annoyed when I see one like that. I don't think they help improve road safety in the least, and it's not at all nice to know that one's children are being brought up with fear (of cars, etc.). You don't want to frighten people, you want to educate them.'

Whether or not this man's views are pertinent is a matter of one's own beliefs on the subject; the fact is that he admitted to being moved by such posters to what may be described as 'acts of social aggression', i.e. every time he saw such posters he either defaced them or, if possible tore them off their mounts.

Next we go on to a general evaluation of the driving test, and specific opinions expressed by the sample interviewed.

Fifty-five motorists were interviewed. Fifty-three suggested they felt the M.O.T. Test to be inadequate.

In what way?

The following comments convey the most common of the attitudes.

[It is] too skimpy – does nothing about night driving.

I took my Test in a three-wheeler, but my licence allows me to drive a motor cycle, about which I haven't the foggiest idea.

When I passed, I was not a competent driver – I wasn't really safe for at least a year afterwards – the Test doesn't account for night driving. . . .

I think questions on the Highway Code and the eye-test are too scant, too casual . . .

A matter of luck really, you should have at least two tests. . . .

More emphasis on stricter driving test rather than new roads, I think it [the Test] is too subjective . . . simulators should be used. . . .

I think it's stupid, no good at all. Anyone can drive well for fifteen or twenty minutes – this is not enough time to make a judgement on, especially in daylight only. . . .

Highway Code should be tested in more detail.

Far too soft [the Test] . . . many people who are passed still haven't the slightest idea how to drive properly. . . .

Made for the 1920s, this is 1966.

They go on and on in the same vein, each opinion voicing a different reason for the modification of the driving test. Some no more than merely academic, most of them pertinent suggestions.

(B) INTERVIEWS WITH PROFESSIONALS

To reiterate, the reasons for interviewing professional people concerned with motoring and its many associated problems were primarily in order to compare their opinions of accident-precipitators with the information already available and, secondly, tentatively to evaluate their attitudes towards traffic legislation and motoring law, with a specific emphasis on their assessment of the driving test.

It is perhaps as well to explain why only certain professionals were interviewed and not some of the more obvious representatives of road associations. Decision against reporting opinions of these latter was made, not arbitrarily, but as a result of certain factors that presented themselves at the outset.

Those representatives of the motoring associations who *were* approached suggested by their attitudes that the investigation in question was really only another vindictive attack on the already over-persecuted motoring population, and implied, if not in so many words, that the writer was best advised to seek information elsewhere. Such loyalty to the motorist is very touching, but hardly progressive.

However, it is certainly doubtful that this is a common malaise. It may have been that the writer was unfortunate in having only contacted unco-operative individuals. Nevertheless, at the time it was felt that other professional opinions would do as well, and hence the final exclusion of motoring association representation.

Members of the police were obviously in a position to furnish relevant details and expert opinions, while driving instructors were in a position to comment on the various types of motorists they encountered in their professional capacity.

Insurance men were interviewed because of the unanimous penalizing of the younger motorist by insurance companies. presumably based on concrete evidence of accident liability in such age-groups. These were the questions in mind during interviews with the motor insurance companies (i.e. specifically which age-groups and what kind of behaviour).

Driving examiners (M.O.T.) were included solely for their assessments of the driving test.

Some specialist opinions have already been mentioned in earlier references to accident-prone motorists, but in order to have a more general indication of the kind of views held by those interviewed, we will treat the opinions of each professional group separately.

The Police

Two inspectors, three sergeants, and six traffic officers were interviewed. Their opinions varied a little in reference to actual offenders within age-groups, but were fairly unanimous about motorists between 17 and 30 years being the chief offenders both in terms of aggressive behaviour and accident liability. In addition, considerable emphasis was placed on the factor of impatience within this age-group.

General feelings expressed suggested that many a conscious effort in the past by the police to improve the present situation in motoring had ended in frustration, usually owing to the very tight and limiting control imposed on them by regulations.

A police inspector (traffic division) made the following comments which he said summed up the overall position: 'I've been concerned with traffic for a good many years now and believe you me, if something isn't done shortly, it will be mass murder on the roads soon. I mean something concrete, something positive. The police should be given a little more authority. I would like to see legislation brought in which enables an officer to ask for and hold a driving licence if he has reason to believe a motorist is a danger to other traffic. At present all one can do is caution a driver and submit a report. The motorist meanwhile is still at large, irrespective of his potential danger to other road users. Such a practice of witholding licences could be a very useful means of discouraging the young, reckless drivers from abusing the privilege of a driving licence by behaving as a lot of them do. Without any hesitation, I would say that most of the accidents I've witnessed in my capacity as a law officer were caused by young people, men, in some aggressive act or another. Trying to do the impossible on the road in a car, taking unnecessary risks, deliberately antagonizing other drivers, complete lack of regard for traffic regulations . . . I could go on and on. It's as though they were sworn to an undertaking of destruction and disruption, whether of traffic regulations, the law, or human life.'

These feelings were strongly expressed and sincerely felt by a man who had seen many tragic consequences of aggression on the roads.

'Why do they have to prove they are better than the other chap?' a police sergeant asked.

Theorists could furnish a variety of reasons, but the point here is not *why* they do it but the fact that they do, and in so doing, frequently turn to aggressive means. One is acutely aware that resentment against youth in terms of motoring is not entirely without a foundation.

Driving Instructors and M.O.T. Examiners

Three instructors and two examiners were interviewed. Owing to the link between the functions of the two professions, opinions expressed will be reported under a joint heading.

Attitudes to aggression on the road were too varied to indicate any representative views apart from a general opinion suggesting, as others before them, that they felt younger motorists *were* apt to be more prone because of 'rashness' on the roads.

The driving test was discussed at length; it transpired that both instructors and examiners were in favour of its revision, and from their manner it was felt that the examiners showed a greater concern for the problem. The illustrations below will convey to the reader some of the views expressed about the interviewees' own positions regarding the driving test.

DRIVING INSTRUCTOR: It is my job and duty to train a person so that he is capable of driving a car properly and with due care and attention to other road-users. Only when I am sure of his capabilities do I suggest that he present himself (or herself) for a test. That's all I can do, but I agree it isn't enough. I cannot change a person's personality, and no matter how efficiently a man uses the controls (of his vehicle) unless he is mentally disciplined as well, he is a potential danger to others. The driving test is made up of situations to assess a driver's ability, his physical judgement, and behaviour only during the Test itself. As it exists, it can do no more than that; immediately on passing the Test a man who has been on his best behaviour during the thirty minutes or so is licensed to drive without anyone knowing what sort of a person he is . . .

M.O.T. EXAMINER: You will find it extremely difficult to get anyone (i.e. examiners) to commit himself, but there are many who feel it's time that something was attempted in making the Test a bit more sophisticated. We are aware that many drivers whom we pass as being capable of handling a vehicle are, in fact, unworthy of the licence given them. But it is not our job to assess any undesirable personality characteristics the examinee possesses. Our suspicions are confined to, and remain, personal beliefs and do not enter into the assessment of driving. People you almost know for certain will misuse the driving licence when given it, come here all dressed up, polite, and on their best driving behaviour. You can only assess them as you see them. If you feel very strongly about their manner you may fail them, but you cannot do such a thing indefinitely . . . the law provides that their 'driving ability' be fairly assessed, and that is all . . . I would certainly encourage any modernization of the prescribed test.

One could say a lot more, but such attitudes as those illustrated above are clear, and much has already been said about the inadequacies of the Test.

Insurance Men

The first question put to them was in connexion with their opinions on the driving test. Again, opinions generally confirmed earlier comments. Next they were asked to explain the policy about higher insurance premiums for younger motorists. There wasn't much explanation to make; facts prompted the constitution of such a policy. Available statistics, their own and others, showed without a doubt that younger motorists *were* a greater liability.

Why?

Mainly because of driving inexperience.

Were there any other factors considered?

Indeed there were; young motorists, it was felt, definitely betrayed obvious signs of dangerous behaviour which only emphasized their accident liability.

In the discussion that followed statements like those above, inevitably the interviewee would produce some 'claims' file and quote examples of such behaviour. The high degree of manifest aggression was very apparent in a considerable number of cases, though occasionally reports made out tended to overlook and oversimplify what actually took place at the time of the accident, in terms of conventional semantics like 'impatience, dangerous driving, lack of consideration, etc.'.

Let us summarize the attitudes of motorists interviewed and the comments of the professionals.

Briefly, there is an indication that young motorists, who have been shown as more aggressive, attempt to justify their anti-social behaviour more readily than to admit such behaviour as adverse to motoring conditions. There is an indication of a mutual dislike between the younger and older age-groups. By the very fact of omission in reference to accident precipitating behaviour, female motorists show a significantly lower degree of accident liability.

Comments made by the professionals interviewed, however briefly reported, indicate that the chief traffic violators have been known for a while, but that existing regulations or legislation offer little hope for the improvement of road safety. Finally, the driving test is in need of some kind of modification if it is to be a useful means of keeping down the number of 'bad' motorists permitted to drive. Let us see how this may best be achieved.

4 Implications

Earlier in the book some suggestions were made concerning more effective means of countering the upward trend in road casualty figures.
Briefly, these were (*i*) that in various parts of the world, specifically
France and America, certain methods and legislation have proved encouraging and could be adopted here, (*ii*) that our own police should be
given authority to hold a driving licence when it is felt that a motorist is a
danger to others and himself, (*iii*) that traffic offences should be dealt with
shortly after the event (this will take a great deal of thinking out), and
(*iv*) that the driving test be modified (and some suggestions were made).

Let us now take again these points, with one or two others.

At present there is almost no way of insuring a high standard of
motoring because of two important factors. First, that the test is inadequate and also that methods of teaching and training would-be motorists vary from Dad teaching Mum on weekends to the rigorous standards
imposed by the better kind of driving school. As far as is known, there
is no 'official' centre where a beginner may receive motoring instruction.

The first problem to be tackled, then, is the setting up all over the
country of official centres for motoring instruction, staffed by instructors who have themselves passed a specified high level course of instruction. There is also a need for all private schools not only to be registered but to have only instructors who had passed this 'official'
instructors' course. This would, of course, mean the disappearance of
the mediocre, only commercially minded driving schools, at present in
their thousands.

Simulator sections attached to 'official' centres of instruction could
be made available at a nominal charge, for the benefit of those would-be
motorists who would rather get the 'feel' of motoring first before attempting an immediate plunge into real traffic. People could still be
permitted to be taught by friends or family members, but they would
not be eligible for a driving test without first having taken a minimum
few hours of instruction from an officially registered instructor.

These suggestions deal only with the beginner. Let us now turn our attention to the man or woman who had managed to fulfil the above requirements (or who is currently a licence-holder) and is later involved in an accident. If the driving test/tests were modified according to earlier suggestions there would be a better basis (using the driver's medical records, etc.) to decide whether it was necessary for the motorist to undergo a re-training programme, psychiatric assessment, or the more conventional systems of fines before a licence is re-issued. People with a record of three or more accidents would automatically become liable for a re-training programme (at an official centre) before being allowed out on the road again.

When it had been proved that a deliberately aggressive act occurred, such as the more dangerous examples illustrated in preceding pages, a minimum period of disqualification would be imposed, followed by the inevitable test, before the re-issue of a licence.

These, together with many earlier ideas, are a general outline of the kind of thinking needed in tackling the problem of driver inadequacy. One other aspect of road safety, vehicle tests, should be made every year, with charges after the first year greatly reduced. There should be spot-checks by the police to maintain a test standard on vehicles at all times, and wider publicity about the penalizing of drivers in 'broken' or dangerously damaged vehicles. In fact, some motorists are reluctant to have necessary car repairs attended to because they fear exploitation by private garages. If there were state-owned garages making nominal charges these drivers would be encouraged to keep their vehicles in good working order.

It is to be hoped that, by a concentrated effort to bring the many aspects of road safety up to date (a constructive basis for modification) some good will result.

EVALUATION OF DATA, AND SUMMARY

We have seen illustrated in this part of the book some aspects of aggression on the roads. Little mention has been made of the influence of anxiety because, apart from a general trend apparent from the analysis of data earlier discussed, little emerged in the course of interviews to warrant any detailed mention of this factor as one potentially dangerous. Additionally, little mention has been made of the woman driver in this section, merely because such views as were expressed by the majority of female motorists interviewed were reasonable, and indicated no need for attaching importance to them as suggesting accident liability.

Women drivers, in short, gave little ground for any acute criticism of attitudes or professed behaviour. They are usually treated uncharitably by males, but in this investigation they emerged as less liable to accidents than most of their menfolk.

So, too, older men, with few exceptions, gave little cause for complaint. It was natural that by concentrating on aggressive and accident-precipitating tendencies much of the content of this book should dwell on the 17–35-year age-group.

In the context of motoring, aggression may be directed at one's own self, at another driver, or at an inanimate object such as a vehicle, a road obstruction, and so on.

High aggression may be seen in one of two ways. Either it may be described as reactive, as when a motorist responds to a particular situation, or it may be termed endogenous (i.e. from within), as when someone is aggressive for no apparent external or logical reason. Both forms can be dangerous, as some examples have demonstrated. General aggressive tendencies appear to be a function of age, significantly decreasing as a person grows older and, presumably, develops a motoring maturity which enables him to curb overtly aggressive acts.

We have observed some illustrations of different ways in which a motorist's aggression finds an outlet. In Part II significant statistics will justify us in suggesting that at a certain particular stage in life a motorist *is* in a particular state of mind that can be distinctly dangerous.

The examples chosen for illustration were more extreme than most, but deliberately so in order to convey a precise indication of the extent to which a motorist can expose his aggression.

What methods are there of combating aggression on the roads? Until some more sophisticated techniques of driver assessment or re-education are established, the chances of effectively controlling road aggression remain only hypothetical. Is it possible to adopt such means of assessment or re-education? Indeed it is, and reference was made to them in the opening pages of this book. The room for increased sophistication is wide – the initiative must be taken. There is little use in making roads wider, surfaces better, traffic signs clearer, and so on, if nothing is done, at least on a basis of equal priority, to establish a minimum level of improved behaviour also.

We are aware that many questions have first to be answered, and more refined methods of research are desirable. Some such questions that spring easily to mind are the following:

(*i*) What are the optimal methods of assessing driving ability (physical, intellectual, emotional) before a licence to drive is issued?

(*ii*) What methods of driver instruction are most likely to succeed in eliminating certain obvious anti-social attitudes?

(*iii*) What are the best methods of re-education for those who are confirmed accident-precipitators?

(*iv*) How best can we make use of propaganda campaigns?

(*v*) What are the most effective ways of helping the police to carry out their tasks?

The arguments for an early initiative, put forward in this book, are admittedly based on a tentative study. Indeed, it is appreciated that even if such proposals *were* taken seriously, the adoption of new means of assessment could be made only gradually over a number of years. It is admitted that, before this happens, more detailed investigations will be necessary.

This book was not written as a conclusive statement or as an academic study. The findings were collated for the interest of those people concerned with making life safer on the highways of Britain. Therefore, of necessity, it is directed to each and every person who assumes the responsibility of taking a vehicle on the road.

PART II

Statistical

5 The study and its background

We have presented in Part I a narrative account of certain qualitative data obtained in this investigation. In this section we shall take a closer look at some of the methodological and technical aspects of the study which, it is hoped, will be of specific value to other people undertaking research into road safety. Such people would of necessity have detailed accounts of the work done by other investigators in the past, so before the quantitative data of this survey are discussed, for the benefit of the interested lay person, it will be useful to look at some of the results obtained by previous workers.

The results, generally speaking, of investigations into the causes of accident-proneness in drivers have only recently started to emerge with any significance. Earlier, results had been far from encouraging. Very little had been conclusively proved regarding the bearing of any one attribute on the accident rate and, indeed, there is still no single specific factor that is psychometrically capable of being identified as a predictor of accident liability.

No sooner did a stated hypothesis appear plausible in the light of investigations carried out than along came another investigator totally opposed to those results, at the same time making his own findings seem equally plausible.

Subsequent work in the study of various other attributes and factors in accident-proneness more or less followed the same pattern of proof and counter-proof. Measures of variables have included those ranging from the purely physiological, through the psycho-physical, to the purely psychological.

Ghiselli and Brown (1948) conducted a study into reaction time and accident-proneness. Their results indicated that short reaction time was associated with low accident figures and that extreme reaction times were very dangerous.

Lauer (1939), on the other hand, had previously done similar work and concluded that short reaction time was associated with high accident rate. Greenshields (1936), Brody (1941), and Häkkinen (1958) concluded there was a lack of evidence to show that reaction times were of any real value in distinguishing between groups of accident-repeaters and accident-free drivers.

With regard to the hypothesis of the influence of intelligence on accident-proneness, according to statements made by Lawshe (1939), drivers having I.Q.s below 75 or 80 and those with I.Q.s between 110 and 125 are dangerous. However, Brody (1941) and Ghiselli (1948), among others, conclude that intelligence has very little bearing on accident-proneness. Again, with regard to certain of the pure physiological investigations, results once more are contradictory. Brody (op. cit.) in his study concluded that low blood-pressure was an important factor in accident-proneness, while Bingham (1931) concluded his investigations in favour of high blood-pressure being the important factor.

It is assumed, then, that tests of this nature are largely valueless in their diagnostic capacity. In fact, it has already been stated that no one test concerned with measuring single attributes is in itself an instrument powerful enough for prediction purposes.

Greater success has been achieved by those administering a 'battery' of tests.

In a study using such techniques, Farmer and Chambers (1939) found that in a group of London bus drivers comparable in respect of age, experience, and type of work done, significant correlation between experience, accidents, and scores in a battery of three 'Aesthetokinetic' (manipulative skill) tests was apparent.

In France, since 1924, when a group of tests designed by Lahy was introduced, Bernard (1952–53) stated that the Paris Transport Organization reported a steady decline in its accident rate per vehicle-mile, and only two years later, in 1926, this had fallen to a quarter of the 1924 figure. It is true that road conditions now are clearly very different from the conditions of 1926, but the fact remains that a battery of tests did have some effect in reducing the accident rate.

Häkkinen (1958) in carrying out similar work in a study of bus and tram drivers in Helsinki, when comparing accident-repeater and accident-free groups, found no significant difference between these groups in attributes such as aptitude, intelligence, tapping rate, simple disjunctive and choice reaction times, biographical data (family status, etc.), attitudes to traffic regulations, and all thirteen variables of a personality inventory used.

The tests which were most successful in separating the two groups were the Multiple Choice reactions or the 'Clock Test', which is a version of Conrad's (1951) Multiple Dial Experiment, using three dials. In this test the subject was, while being distracted, required to keep a pointer over a moving wavy line with the aid of a steering wheel and foot pedals.

Other tests of some significance in the 'battery' were eye–hand co-ordination, the number of motor disturbances during wrong and correct reactions on a Psychomotor personality test modelled on Davis's Skilled Response Test. In both the Myokinetic Psychodiagnostic (MPI) or Mira Tests, and the Body Sway Test (a Test of Suggestibility), the accident group was also shown to be more unstable and emotionally labile. In his conclusions Häkkinen indicated that motor (i.e. physical) hastiness and distractibility gave rise to accident-proneness.

Davis and Coiley (1959), in their study on accident-proneness, classified each subject on the basis of known accident records, i.e. for every 100,000 vehicle-miles driven. Those with three or more accidents were classified as accident-prone and those with a lower rate as safe. This method of classification, however, is still too vague a measure for purposes of prediction. Account must be taken of frequency and duration of frequency at each driving attempt. Number of miles driven are in themselves valueless.

The importance of personality and temperament is not overlooked either, and in fact is considered as extremely significant in connexion with accident-proneness.

Davis (1948), using an elaborate apparatus designed by Craik and Drew, classified air pilots into three groups.

(*i*) Those showing inertia, characterized by lack of attention, lowering of standards, tiredness, and emotional difficulties.

(*ii*) Those showing over-activity, tenseness, and irritability.

(*iii*) Those showing normal reactions to the complex situation.

In a follow-up study those in groups (*i*) and (*ii*) were found to be more frequently suspended and to be involved in proportionately more fatal accidents.

By far one of the more interesting studies in the last twenty years has been that of Dunbar (1944), in which (unintentionally) she discovered the importance of personality to accident-proneness. For a personality investigation of patients suffering from cardiovascular disease, she chose as a control group patients in a fracture ward. She found them unsatis-factory for her purpose because most of them possessed abnormal personality traits in common. The group was characterized by a good health record, a history of previous accidents, a high family divorce rate, a tendency for individuals to be in conflict with authority and to show aggressive self-reliance, and to have many and varied jobs.

McFarland (1957), and a number of other investigators, partly upheld the view that accident-repeaters react against authority, have aggressive tendencies, are irresponsible, and are likely to be socially maladjusted.

It will be shown later how findings in this study further indicate the relationship between aggressive tendencies and accident liability. In conclusion, then, it appears that data in respect of temperament, etc. are certainly significant enough to take seriously. As expressed in the words of *Research on Road Safety* (Road Research Laboratories, 1963): '. . . If this general picture of the accident-prone temperament is correct, it is important to consider whether practical use can be made of test results to get rid of, or re-educate, those drivers suspected of accident-proneness . . .'

THE PRELIMINARY STUDY (A)

The scope for investigation was enormous. Getting motorists to co-operate was by no means difficult, though the limitations of the study as imposed by financial and other considerations were very precise. However, mention has been made of this in preceding pages.

The first step was the design of the study, and this was broken down into progressive stages as follows:

(1) Formulating basic concepts of Aggression and Anxiety with respect to motoring. For purposes of this survey, it was felt that the only way to arrive at a representative list that classified items of behaviour or attitudes under Aggression and Anxiety would be to enlist the help of the motorists themselves; in other words, to get motorists to say what *they* considered aggressive and anxious behaviour to be.

Accordingly, a random sample of drivers ($N = 50$) was drawn. The drivers of one in every Nth vehicle to pass a given point became eligible. The site was carefully chosen on a major road into London, where all types of vehicles were available and where, owing to the daily traffic-jam, both local and out-of-town drivers could be easily approached.

They were briefly told that the survey was being carried out to find out about attitudes to motoring. If they agreed to take part they were asked to take home two sheets of paper (headed *aggression* and *anxiety*) and list on them what they considered to be aggressive and anxious behaviour or attitudes to motoring (within the motoring situation).

In addition, friends and acquaintances were also approached with the same request.

The response was very encouraging. After eliminating any responses on grounds of ambiguity or irrelevancy, the final number of items (65) was used as a basis for formulating the aggression and anxiety traits.

An interesting observation made using this method of approach (i.e one in every *N*th vehicle) strongly indicates, with few exceptions, that motorists are extremely eager to impart their views on driving to others, for the success rate of replies received was 72% (36 out of 50 drivers approached).

This is especially high when one considers that they were requested to post their responses back to the writer and only a very few stamped envelopes were provided. Future researchers using this method of sampling should note that indications are that an apologetic though serious approach stressing the importance of the subject's views will be most successful. An old college scarf helps if you have one!

The breakdown of the 36 random sample motorists and 14 friends is shown in *Table 1*.

Table 1

Breakdown of drivers used for basic
AG/AN behaviour formulation

Type of vehicle	No. of drivers	Male	Female
Cars	21	17	4
Trucks	7	7	—
Vans	4	4	—
M/Cycles	2	2	—
Others *	2	1	1
Totals	36	31	5
Plus friends (car-drivers)	14	8	6
Grand total	50	39	11

* Bubble-cars, invalid carriages, etc.

(2) On the basis of the responses given by motorists with regard to AG/AN behaviour, etc. (see Section 1 above), a preliminary list was

prepared with a total of 65 AG items and 38 AN items (both pertaining to behaviour and attitudes).

In the numerous 'brain-storming' sessions which followed, the list was reduced to 50 AG items and 25 AN items. These sessions were held with people believed to be most qualified in vetting the final list, namely, police officers, driving instructors, and psychologists. In a final attempt to insure against any important or relevant item being over-looked, the list was passed for scrutiny to some police drivers on the assumption that they were perhaps the most qualified observers of driver behaviour in all kinds of situations. Nothing new was added.

While many of those who took part in the first compilation of aggressive and anxious behaviour included items pertaining to alcohol or to 'drinking and driving', it was felt that these items should be excluded from any subsequent lists. This was mainly because the 'behaviour' studied here was explicitly that kind of behaviour which was 'spontaneous' in the driving situation, without the influence of alcohol or other stimulants. It can be argued that driving after drinking is 'normal' behaviour with some people, and should therefore be included as being part of the whole driving situation. However, not all those 'under the influence' are aggressive when driving, hence any assumption that 'drinking and driving' constitutes aggressive behaviour would be quite incorrect.

No separate list of the final 75 items used in the survey has been included in these pages, since they are the same items as appear in the questionnaire set out in Appendix I.

THE PRELIMINARY STUDY (B)

As before, the sample was obtained by selecting a stretch along a major road into London for its density and convergence of traffic from many and varied geographical areas. Once again, the driver of every *N*th vehicle to pass within the chosen stretch was approached.

The traffic flow here was faster than at the spot used for obtaining the AG/AN formulation sample, but still slow enough (at the rush hour) to enable the writer to approach the motorists. It was found convenient to use every tenth vehicle.

Sixty questionnaires for distribution were prepared together with self-addressed envelopes. In addition, an explanatory note pertaining to the survey was included with each. The distribution itself was made over two days, the first day in the morning and the second day in the evening. This was done for reasons of convenience only.

The 75 items within the questionnaire, of which only 45 (i.e. 30 AG and 15 AN) were required, were subsequently the same as used in the main-study questionnaire. At this stage, however, they were not placed according to any specially randomized order (see Questionnaire, main study, p. 76).

Of the 60 questionnaires handed out, 41 (68·3%) were returned filled in, though only 25 (41·6%) of these were of any use. The others were inadequately completed (i.e. not all 75 items were attempted). However, as the writer had envisaged the use of approximately 30 (50%) completed questionnaires for preliminary work, the above figure was quite satisfactory. Distribution of the 25 drivers is shown in *Tables 2a* and *2b*.

Table 2a

Breakdown of drivers used in pilot study

Group	Age	Total No.	Male	Female
I	17y–24y 6m	3	2	1
II	24y 7m–34y 6m	6	4	2
III	34y 7m–44y 6m	8	5	3
IV	44y 7m–54y 6m	4	2	2
V	54y 7m–64y 6m	3	2	1
VI	64y 7m–74y 6m	1	1	—
	Totals	25	16 (64%)	9 (36%)

Table 2b

Classification of drivers in age-groups and type of vehicle driven (preliminary study)

Type of vehicle	Age-groups *						Totals
	I	II	III	IV	V	VI	
Car	1	4	5	4	3	1	18
Lorry	1	1	1	—	—	—	3
Van	—	1	2	—	—	—	3
M/Cycle	1	—	—	—	—	—	1
Totals	3	6	8	4	3	1	25

* See *Table 2a*.

Figure 1
Rank order AG frequency of 25 motorists in preliminary study

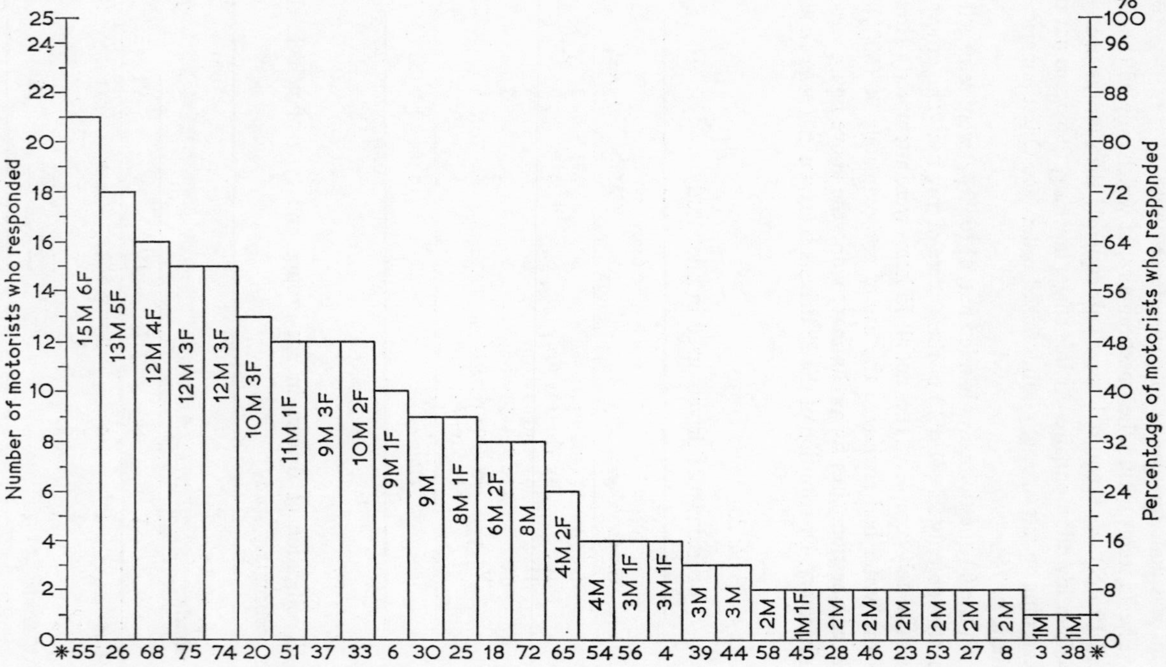

Percentage of motorists who responded

%
100 96 88 80 72 64 56 48 40 32 24 16 8 0

Number of motorists who responded

25 24 22 20 18 16 14 12 10 8 6 4 2 0 *

Bar	Value
15M 6F	55
13M 5F	26
12M 4F	68
12M 3F	75
12M 3F	74
10M 3F	20
11M 1F	51
9M 3F	37
10M 2F	33
9M 1F	6
9M	30
8M 1F	25
6M 2F	18
8M	72
4M 2F	65
4M 1F	56
4M	54
3M 1F	4
3M 1F	39
3M	44
3M	58
2M	45
1M1F	28
2M	46
2M	23
2M	53
2M	27
2M	8
1M	3
1M	38

* See Appendix III for interpretation of these items.

With the exception of a single respondent, all other questionnaires were completed without any remarks to indicate that instructions given were inadequate. The only remark suggested that the subject was not sure whether he was supposed to respond to the item given as an example. This was clarified in the main study, though (perhaps owing to over-zealousness or just not reading the instructions fully) many respondents continued to indicate their choice of alternatives in the 'example' item as well!

Letters were written to the 19 drivers who did not return their questionnaires, to find out why they had not done so. Only 6 replied; some indicated that they hadn't sufficient time, and one, a woman, that some of the items were impertinent! She had enclosed the questionnaire with red pencil rings around items that had presumably offended her, 'Women drivers are not as good as men drivers', 'Women drivers are more nervous than men drivers', 'I never swear at other drivers'.

BRIEF ANALYSIS AND PRESENTATION OF DATA IN PRELIMINARY STUDY

As *Figure 1* indicates, the most common aggressive behaviour relates to item 55,* 'Swearing' (though not out loud) at other drivers. This seems to be true for both male and female drivers. In fact, as shown in the graphical representation (*Figure 2*), the tendencies for responses of AG behaviour, etc., against the 30 variables are pretty similar in the two groups.

An interesting observation is that, while at least 50% of the male drivers admit to 'cutting across if in the wrong lane of traffic', not a single female does so. This, of course, could mean that even though the men have a tendency towards 'cutting across', it does not necessarily follow that it is done without heed to traffic. On the other hand, this could also indicate, with certain individuals, that the tendency towards 'cutting across' in traffic is not a premeditated act, taking into account the safety margin for doing so, but (and perhaps in keeping within a pattern of aggressive driving behaviour) the sign of an impulsive or impatient nature translated into the driving situation *without* heed to other traffic.

The lack of any female driver to respond in the same manner could be due to higher anxiety while driving (see *Figure 4*) and consequently greater caution. With a sample of only nine female motorists, an assumption like this can be no more than tentative.

* See Appendix I, p. 124.

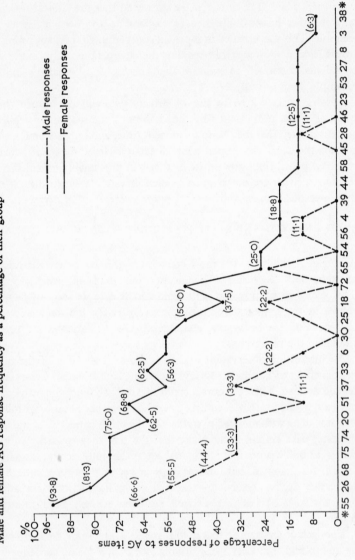

Figure 2
Male and female AG response frequency as a percentage of their group

— — — Male responses
——— Female responses

* *See Figure 1.*

70

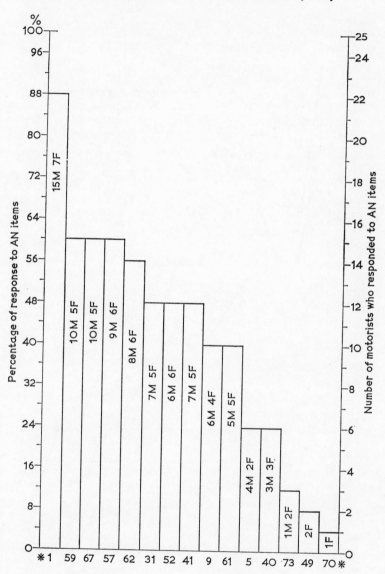

Figure 3

Rank order of AN frequencies of 25 motorists in preliminary study

* See Appendix III for interpretation of these items.

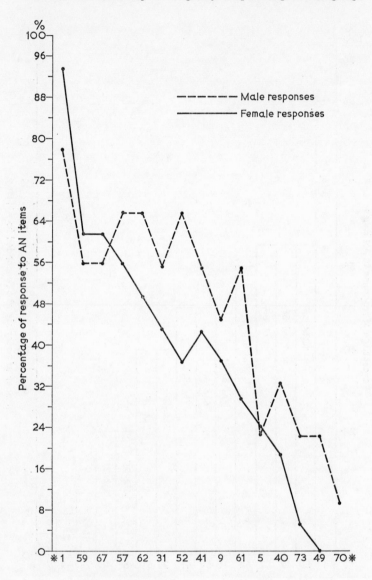

Figure 4

Male and female AN response frequency as a percentage of their group

* See Appendix III for interpretation of these items.

72

At this stage nothing more than a breakdown of the frequencies of AG and AN responses was attempted, but even from such little information one cannot help noticing that a sample of no more than 25 motorists indicated the greater element of Aggression present in males and the interesting tendency of women to be more Anxious in the driving situation – interesting in so far as this kind of 'image' of the woman driver rather conforms to attitudes generally prevalent in our society.

One can readily see from *Figure 2* that the tendency for responses in both male and female drivers is similar with regard to any specific AG items. *Figure 4* indicates this similarity in reverse; *Figures 5* and *6* show each motorist's AG score against the AN score and the coefficient of correlation, *r*. (In the preliminary stage scoring was done on a simple basis of one point credited per AG/AN item chosen by the motorist.)

From *Figure 5* we may observe $r = +0.75$, thus showing a tendency for male aggression scores to be functionally associated with their anxiety scores in a positive manner (high aggression is usually indicative of high anxiety, and vice versa). In *Figure 6*, $r = -0.78$, here the tendency is of a negative nature, indicating that the high aggression scores of women are related to low anxiety scores.

No attempt was made to see if there was any AG/AN correlation with accidents, the figures of which are given in *Table 3* below. The accidents were simply reported as Very Serious, Serious, or Minor, and no provision was made for recording the number of each if there was more than one of a kind.

Table 3

Accidents reported by drivers in the preliminary study questionnaire

Number of drivers	*Accident (type)*		
	Very serious	*Serious*	*Minor*
Male (N = 16)	1	3	4
Female (N = 9)	—	1	3
Totals	1	4	7

Criteria for the constitution of each type of accident were left to the discretion of the individual respondent, and checked for consistency with the interview sample of motorists. (No significant reclassification

Figure 5
Correlation between male AG and AN scores (preliminary study)

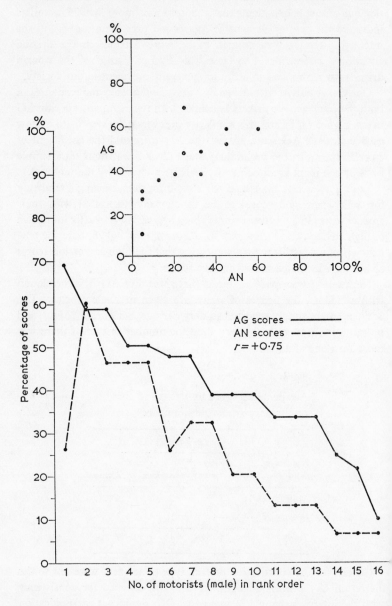

Figure 6
Correlation between female AG and AN scores (preliminary study)

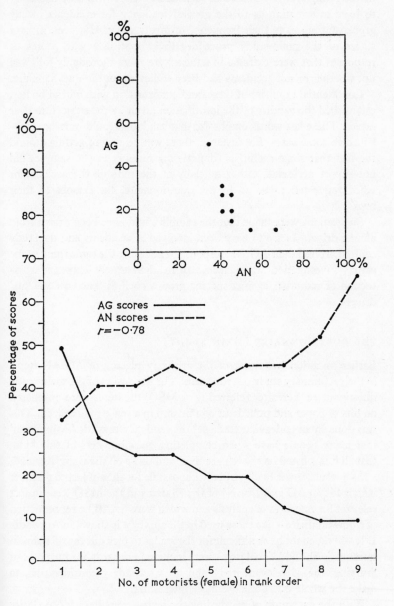

was necessary.) As the study was being undertaken with a view to investigating AG/AN behaviour (attitudes, etc.), it was only necessary to have information as to the general tendency for accidents in any group and not as to their frequency of involvement. However, in later stages of the main-study procedure those motorists with scores or responses that were extreme in nature were more thoroughly followed up, whether or not accidents had been indicated on the questionnaire.

Confidential inquiries of these, and confirmation with official bodies, established the validity of the information given by the subject, *to some extent*. These last words emphasize that validation could only be established in some cases. For instance, there was no way of getting around the fact that some motorists (doubtless a number in the sample) did not report accidents, either officially at the time of the accident or when requested to do so in the questionnaire, for reasons of their own.

Suggestions were made that the sample could have been drawn from among drivers *known* to have been involved in accidents and the study centred around their AG/AN responses – not quite the same thing as the actual investigation undertaken, which deliberately chose a cross-section of motorists against specific groups such as 'known accidents' drivers.

THE QUESTIONNAIRE (MAIN STUDY)

Earlier, mention was made of the arbitrary placing of AG/AN items in the preliminary study questionnaire. For the design of the main study questionnaire (hereafter referred to as MSQ) the items were numbered on bits of paper and pulled out of a tin and in a sense randomized. This was done in an endeavour to dispel the tendency towards 'assumption' that many people have when completing questionnaires of this kind, that all items listed on the left are 'For' and those on the right 'Against'.

As a result, it was made virtually impossible for the subject to discover which 45 (30 AG and 15 AN) of the 75 items in the MSQ were in fact relevant for purposes of analysis and which were not. (The reproduction of a questionnaire – like those used in the survey – is shown in Appendix I. It will no doubt be as difficult for the reader to pick out the 45 items in question.) The additional items were included primarily for purposes of 'burying' the 45 relevant items and, as a secondary consideration, to make the whole questionnaire more interesting.

With the exception of re-wording the instructions in order to clarify what was required of the respondent, no alterations were made in the items themselves in the MSQ.

In the Personal Details section, however, added information was requested in the form of 'marital status' and 'educational background', though data from the latter was not analysed owing to gross omissions by respondents. Provision was also made for including 'convictions' for specific offences such as speeding.

6 Samples and sampling methods

It has been shown why decisions were made against the use of the electoral register and, because it was unobtainable, the current list of registered driving-licence holders. Above, mention was made of the use of three different means of obtaining motorists to make up the whole sample. They were as follows:

METHODS EMPLOYED

(i) Random sampling

With the use of random number tables, 229 motorists (male and female) were contacted by calling at a proportional number of houses on every road in the area from which the sample was to be drawn.

For the benefit of those who stress the importance of the influence of social classification on motoring behaviour, as the district chosen has its share of residential sections along the continuum from rich to poor socio-economic dwellings, the sample of motorists obtained in this manner was fairly cross-sectional. Of the 229 drivers contacted by random means, 108 agreed to take part; from these, 102 questionnaires were used, a few being omitted from the study as they were not fully completed (see *Table 4*).

Table 4

102 motorists in sample I (random selection) main study, in age-groups

Group *	Male	Female	Totals
I	20	10	30
II	24	7	31
III	11	8	19
IV	11	2	13
V	7	1	8
VI	1	—	1
Totals	74	28	102

* Group I 17y to 24y 6m
II 24y 7m to 34y 6m
III 34y 7m to 44y 6m
IV 44y 7m to 54y 6m
V 54y 7m to 64y 6m
VI 64y 7m to 74y 6m

(ii) One in N number of vehicles to pass a given point

It has already been mentioned that part of the main study sample was obtained in a manner similar to previous samples in the survey.

A major road in the borough was chosen, for the same reasons as before, i.e. convergence of traffic and rush-hour traffic jams, when consequently easier approaches to motorists could be made.

Earlier in the chapter, reference was made to a decision against obtaining the whole sample in this way. This decision was taken for the following reason. A major disadvantage would have been one of obtaining a cross-section of motorists with reference to driving frequency; the preliminary samples drawn from one in N motorists having shown that a very high percentage of them were regular daily drivers. On the assumption that motorists who drive daily have differences in attitude to motoring as against those who drive only occasionally, it was felt that some additional means was required of including 'less frequent' motorists in the sample. In spite of precautions, however, the sample was nevertheless made up mostly of 'daily' motorists (72·8%) (see table in Appendix II).

Of the 175 approached, 143 (see *Table 5*) contributed to the total of the overall sample.

Table 5

143 motorists in sample II (one in N selection) main study, in age-groups

Group	Male	Female	Totals
I	29	14	43
II	35	9	44
III	15	11	26
IV	15	3	18
V	10	2	12
VI	—	—	—
Totals	104	39	143

(iii) Self-selective sample

For obvious administrative advantages this method of sampling was the most rewarding, although the decision to use it was not made solely on the basis of personal convenience.

In fact, while it was convenient for the questionnaires not to be personally distributed as a result of permitting a self-selective sample, the author spent many a precious evening having to read through and discard a substantial number of over-zealous and anecdotal responses from the 180 questionnaires received. The procedure for obtaining the sample was devised in the following way:

Piles of questionnaires were left at local public libraries, in factory canteens, and schools, etc., with an explanatory note about the survey displayed near by. Those interested were requested to take a questionnaire from the pile, and after completing it were asked either to return it by post or to leave it with an appointed named person. No time limit was given, but subjects were requested to return their completed questionnaires as soon as possible.

Addressed envelopes were not provided, the rationale being that all participants would be genuinely interested in the survey, thus eliminating a great number of unnecessary responses from those people who fill in questionnaires just for the sake of it!

The 137 subjects used from the 180 responses are shown in *Table 6*.

Table 6

137 motorists in sample III (self-selection) main study, in age-groups

Group	Male	Female	Totals
I	28	12	40
II	33	9	42
III	15	11	26
IV	14	2	16
V	10	1	11
VI	1	1	2
Totals	101	36	137

Table 7

382 motorists in overall sample (main study), in age-groups

Group	Male	Female	Totals
I	77	36	113
II	92	25	117
III	41	30	71
IV	40	7	47
V	27	4	31
VI	2	1	3
Totals	279	103	382

Figure 7a

Plotted points of frequencies in Table 8a

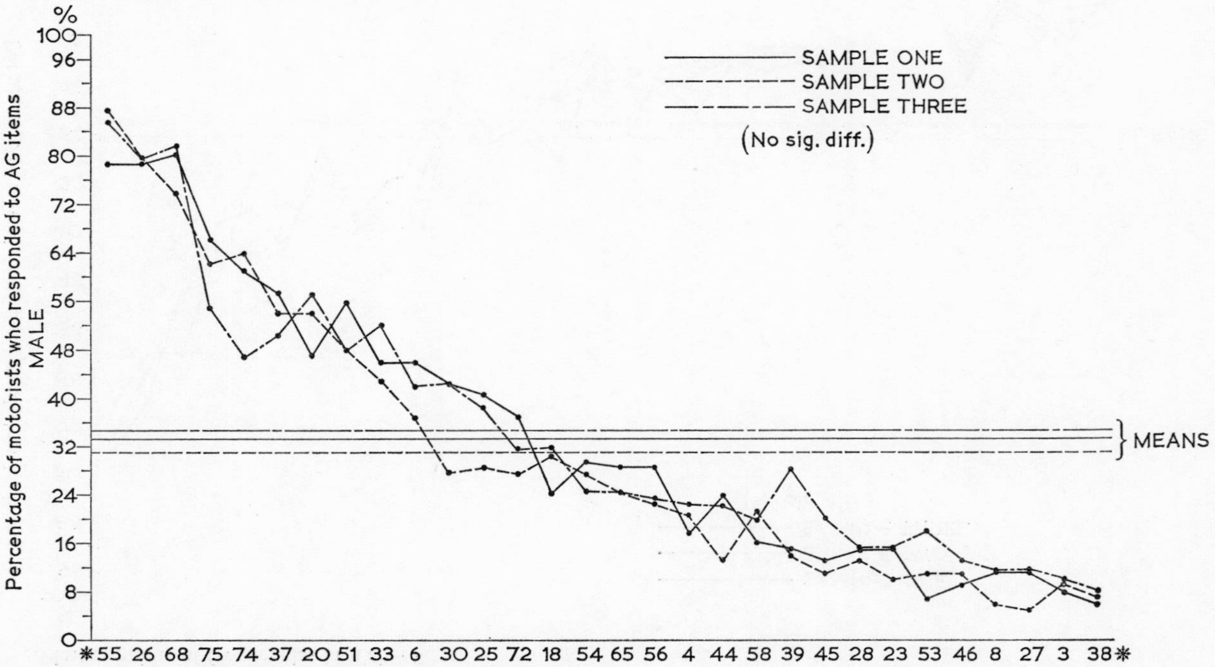

SAMPLE ONE
SAMPLE TWO
SAMPLE THREE

(No sig. diff.)

Percentage of motorists who responded to AG items

MALE

% 100 96 88 80 72 64 56 48 40 32 24 16 8 O

MEANS

* 55 26 68 75 74 37 20 51 33 6 30 25 72 18 54 65 56 4 44 58 39 45 28 23 53 46 8 27 3 38 *

* See Appendix III for interpretation of these items.

81

Figure 7b

Plotted points of frequencies in Table 8b

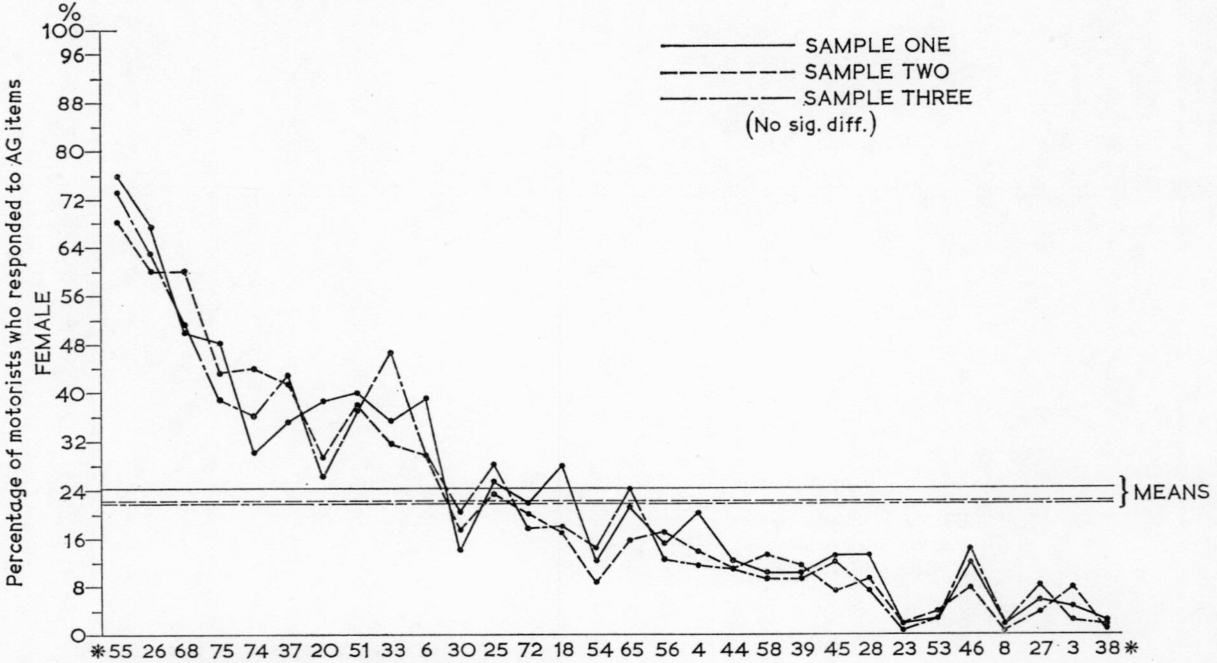

SAMPLE ONE
SAMPLE TWO
SAMPLE THREE
(No sig. diff.)

} MEANS

Percentage of motorists who responded to AG items

FEMALE

* 55 26 68 75 74 37 20 51 33 6 30 25 72 18 54 65 56 4 44 58 39 45 28 23 53 46 8 27 3 38 *

* See Appendix III for interpretation of these items.

82

Figure 8

Plotted points of sample mean frequencies in Tables 8a and 8b

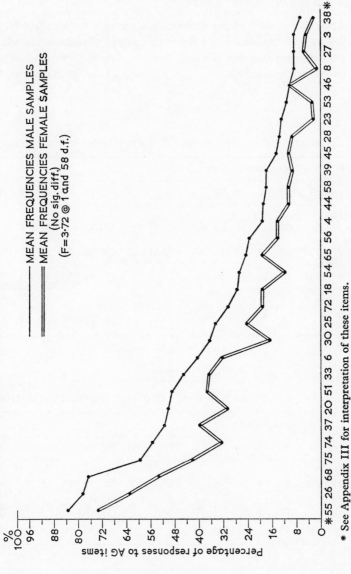

MEAN FREQUENCIES MALE SAMPLES

MEAN FREQUENCIES FEMALE SAMPLES
(No sig. diff.)
($F = 3.72$ @ 1 and 58 d.f.)

Percentage of responses to AG items

% 100 96 88 80 72 64 56 48 40 32 24 16 8 0

* 55 26 68 75 74 37 20 51 33 6 30 25 72 18 54 65 56 4 44 58 39 45 28 23 53 46 8 27 3 38 *

* See Appendix III for interpretation of these items.

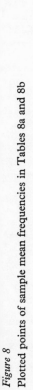

83

DISCUSSION OF METHODS

Owing to the lack of any statistical control over the way in which the last sample was obtained, a reasonable degree of concern was felt with regard to any bias that this lack may have caused in the data collected. However, in reiterating and emphasizing an earlier statement, there

Table 8a

Percentage distribution of male frequency responses to AG items in

Male samples	AG items*														
	55	26	68	75	74	37	20	51	33	6	30	25	72	18	54
One N = 74	78	78	79	65	60	56	46	55	45	45	42	40	36	24	29
Two N = 104	87	79	73	61	63	53	53	47	42	36	27	28	27	30	27
Three N = 101	85	78	80	54	46	47	56	47	51	41	42	38	31	31	24
Means of AG items †	83	78	77	60	56	52	51	50	46	41	37	35	31	28	27

Table 8b

Percentage distribution of female frequency responses to AG items in

Female samples	AG items*														
	55	26	68	75	74	37	20	51	33	6	30	25	72	18	54
One N = 28	76	67	50	48	30	35	38	40	35	39	14	25	22	28	12
Two N = 39	68	60	60	43	44	41	29	38	31	30	17	23	20	21	9
Three N = 36	73	63	51	39	36	43	26	37	46	30	20	28	17	18	14
Means of AG items †	73	63	54	43	33	40	31	38	37	33	17	25	20	20	12

* See Appendix III for interpretation of these items.   † Rounded.

were found to be no statistically significant differences between them when the three samples were subjected to the usual statistical procedures, and the customary Analysis of Variance* was carried out.

Tables 8a and *8b* and *Figures 7a* and *7b* numerically and graphically present the frequencies of responses of these three samples to the questionnaire AG items.

rank order (main study)

65	56	4	44	58	39	45	28	23	53	46	8	27	3	38	*Mean frqcy†*
28	28	17	24	16	15	13	15	15	7	9	11	11	8	6	33
24	22	20	13	21	14	11	13	10	11	11	6	5	9	7	31
24	23	22	22	20	28	20	15	15	18	13	11	11	10	8	34
25	24	20	20	19	19	15	14	13	12	11	9	9	9	7	

rank order (main study)

65	56	4	44	58	39	45	28	23	53	46	8	27	3	38	*Mean frqcy †*
21	15	20	12	10	10	13	13	2	3	12	2	6	5	3	24
16	17	14	11	13	11	7	9	2	4	8	1	4	8	1	22
24	12	11	11	9	9	12	7	1	3	14	1	8	2	2	22
20	15	15	11	11	10	11	10	2	3	11	1	6	5	2	

* For a very explicit introduction to analysis of variance the reader unfamiliar with statistics is recommended to read *Facts from Figures* (Moroney, 1965).

It may be noted that the AG means of the samples with regard to response frequency of both male and female motorists are very similar. The same pattern – which one would expect after noting the similarities of AG responses – is confirmed by the sample responses to AN items in the questionnaire (see *Tables 9a* and *9b* and *Figure 9*).

Table 9a
Percentage distribution of male frequency responses to AN items in rank order (main study)

Male samples	AN items *															Mean frqcy†
	1	67	59	57	62	31	41	52	61	9	5	73	49	40	70	
One N = 74	66	79	41	47	41	25	28	23	18	15	14	16	18	6	0	29
Two N = 104	71	38	43	40	37	25	15	19	18	15	17	11	8	11	0	25
Three N = 101	65	54	43	38	25	25	28	29	20	11	8	6	18	8	1	25
Means of AN items †	67	57	42	42	34	25	24	24	19	14	13	11	15	8	0	

Table 9b
Percentage distribution of female frequency responses to AN items in rank order (main study)

Female samples	AN items *															Mean frqcy†
	1	67	59	57	62	31	41	52	61	9	5	73	49	40	70	
One N = 28	60	54	47	35	33	25	32	27	26	28	38	21	15	27	4	32
Two N = 39	65	60	42	48	32	26	29	20	29	21	39	15	11	31	2	31
Three N = 36	58	45	48	38	36	24	27	30	18	26	34	19	12	25	3	30
Means of AN items †	61	50	46	40	34	25	29	26	24	25	37	18	13	28	3	

* See Appendix III for interpretation of these items.
† Rounded.

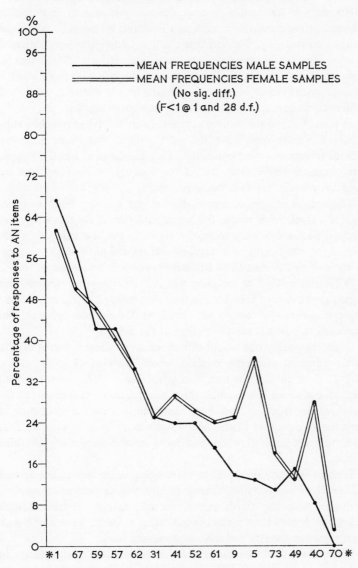

Figure 9

Plotted points of sample mean frequencies in Tables 9a and 9b

MEAN FREQUENCIES MALE SAMPLES
MEAN FREQUENCIES FEMALE SAMPLES
(No sig. diff.)
(F<1 @ 1 and 28 d.f.)

Percentage of responses to AN items

*1 67 59 57 62 31 41 52 61 9 5 73 49 40 70 *

* See Appendix III for interpretation of these items.

87

This is very interesting indeed, especially when consideration is given to the varying methods used in obtaining the samples.

However, in attempting to treat the available data in an objective manner, before certain inferences may be drawn we begin by taking the samples individually. We find that the first sample was – as indicated above – obtained by using standard statistical methods of randomness. This was done by using random-number tables as a basis from which a proportionate number of houses in the sampling area were called at, and motorists, when contacted, asked to fill in a questionnaire.

In order to keep the sample as 'pure' (statistically) as possible, subsidiary lists were kept, using the same method, and where necessary substitute subjects were contacted. This emphasizes that the sample was obtained wholly from within the Borough of Hornsey with no apparent outside influence being present.

The second sample involved stopping one in every tenth motorist to pass a given point within the borough. Again, if the tenth motorist stopped declined to participate, the eleventh was also stopped, which altered the numbering procedure, so that instead of the next tenth car to come along the next ninth one was approached, and so on.

While this method of sampling was in itself somewhat random with regard to the type of vehicles and motorists stopped, it did not exclude those motorists approached who lived outside the borough but who happened to pass the sampling point at the time.

Quite reasonably one would expect results to show a degree of bias in the adoption of such a method, which included 43 motorists (or 30·1%) from outside the area – in other words 11·3% of the overall sample. But as the above tables show, the frequency of response to the questionnaire items did not vary significantly from the frequency of response of motorists in the first – statistically 'pure' – sample. This is further emphasized when one looks at the results of the third sample.

If there was any doubt as to there being some bias in the second sample, there was every justification in expecting an element of sampling prejudice with the third. Again, though, results repudiated such beliefs; responses from motorists indicating a similar pattern of choice with regard to the AG and AN questionnaire items.

What, then, could be the reason for there being no differences in responses in the light of such diverse methods of sampling? Below are listed certain hypotheses:

(*i*) Owing to the fact that most of the motorists in the overall sample were from the same area (i.e. living in the same borough), attitudes to motoring were similar because of certain local influences.

(*ii*) The kind of motoring required in urban areas influences a particular attitude to motoring, and as almost all those in the sample lived in and around London, responses to the questionnaire items were similar.

(*iii*) There is *no real* difference in general attitudes to motoring whether one lives in town or not; thus responses of a group of motorists, such as those who took part in the survey, are typical of the responses that can be expected from all motorists, and therefore reflect a national pattern of driving behaviour.

All of the above statements are plausible, but all are still unproven. If the first is to be studied one would have to undertake an investigation using the same questionnaires and methods of sampling in various parts of the country in order to prove or disprove the hypothesis. However, a research into differences other than social background would require investigation, for it has already been pointed out that the area in Hornsey from which the sample was drawn had varying social structures within it which resulted in a fairly cross-sectional sample in respect to socio-economic status.

In order to establish whether the second statement is true, one would have to study differences between change in attitudes from urban to rural motoring (or vice versa), again in different parts of the country. Finally, if the third statement is to be accepted, then one could confidently say that there is a uniformity of driving attitudes and behaviour in the motoring situation within the British Isles, and that Aggressive and Anxious responses are not influenced by general social or cultural factors.

Before leaving the discussion on sampling and sampling methods it is perhaps worth taking a final look at the results to see how closely they resemble the pattern of responses obtained from the very few motorists in the preliminary study.

It may be seen from *Figure 2* (page 70) that responses to the AG items on the questionnaire by the 16 male motorists in the preliminary study are fairly similar to the responses given by the 279 males in the main study (see *Figure 10*).

Indeed, one may ask whether it is possible for the responses of a mere score of motorists to be fairly indicative of the responses to be expected

Figure 10

Similarities of responses to AG items between 16 male motorists in the
preliminary study and 279 male motorists in the main study

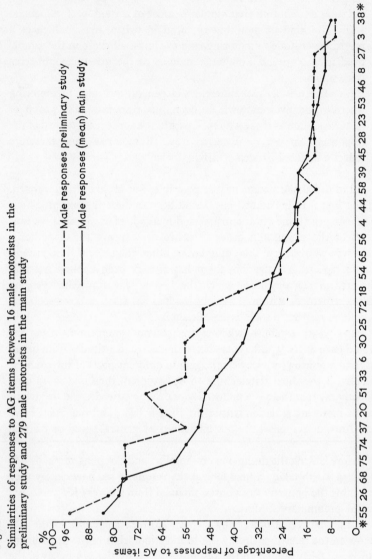

----- Male responses preliminary study

——— Male responses (mean) main study

Percentage of responses to AG items

* 55 26 68 75 74 37 20 51 33 6 30 25 72 18 54 65 56 4 44 58 39 45 28 23 53 46 8 27 3 38 *

* See Appendix III for interpretation of these items.

Figure 11
Age distribution as a percentage of the whole sample (main study)

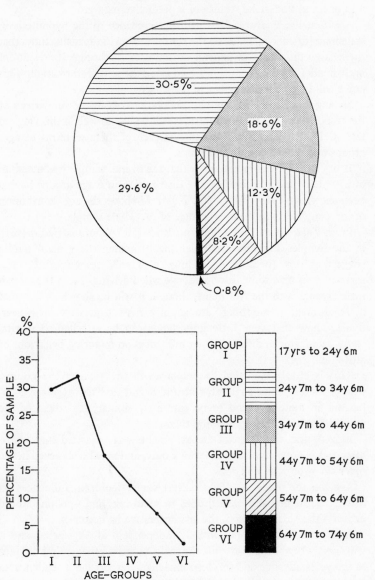

from a much larger group. If this is so only a handful of motorists would be needed – as long as they were fairly cross-sectional in age, etc. – in order to undertake studies of a predictive nature.

Additionally, this would give further credence to the hypothesis in statement (iii), above, made on the results of data in the main study, that there is *no* difference in general attitudes to motoring, the results of both smaller and larger samples conveying the same information. This point will be discussed further in later pages.

Having made some interesting observations about the similarities of the responses in the three samples, it will be just as well at this stage to take a closer look at what constituted each of them in terms of age-groups and other defining categories.

It has already been pointed out that the overall sample was made up of 279 males and 103 females, the distribution into age-groups having been shown in *Table 7* (page 80). *Figure 11* shows the age distribution of the sample drivers as a percentage of the whole sample.

From *Table 10* we find a high incidence (60·7%) of married drivers in the sample. There is a popular theory among the general public suggesting that (because of feelings of family responsibility, etc.) married men tend to be less aggressive when driving. From the overall male responses to the AG items, though, it will be shown in fact that married men, if anything, are slightly *more* aggressive. However, figures show that very little importance can be attached to marital status as a factor in differentiating influences on motoring behaviour or attitudes.

This is clearly indicated by responses in the younger age-groups, where, for example, aggressive attitudes and attested aggressive behaviour in motoring tend to be extremely similar, regardless of the marital status of those professing them.

Indeed, the similarity of behaviour between married and other motorists is not confined to the young only, and may be observed in the older age-groups as well.

Age, on the other hand, does exert some significant influences on driving behaviour and on attitudes to motoring, and – as one would expect – the older a person, the less aggressive he becomes.

Anxiety is, however, not entirely independent of Aggression, and it will shortly be shown that while the male motorist becomes less anxious as the years advance on him, his female counterpart has a tendency to become more anxious in later life.

Table 10

Breakdown of marital status within age-groups (main study sample)

Group	Sex	Single	Married	Other*	Totals
I	M	64	13	—	77
	F	25	10	1	36
II	M	27	64	1	92
	F	8	15	2	25
III	M	3	37	1	41
	F	8	20	2	30
IV	M	2	37	1	40
	F	—	7	—	7
V	M	1	26	—	27
	F	1	1	2	4
VI	M	—	2	—	2
	F	—	—	1	1
Totals	M	97	179	3	} 382
	F	42	53	8	
Percentage		(36·4)	(60·7)	(2·9)	(100)

* i.e. Divorced, separated, widowed.

SCORING

As there were only 30 AG items and 15 AN items required from the questionnaire for purposes of analysis, no importance was attached to those responses given to the other thirty items whose inclusion in the questionnaire was explained earlier.

The scoring method was simple and uniform in its application and derived by the following procedure. If, for example, a motorist chose the Aggressive box, of the two alternatives given, in response to a statement on the questionnaire (i.e. he '*did* swear' at other motorists) he was given a basic AG score of 1 for that choice. Similarly, if he chose the Anxiety

H

box of the two alternatives he was given a basic AN score of 1 for that choice also.

In addition, each of the total 45 items (30 AG and 15 AN) was given a subsidiary score which was derived by dividing the total sample response to that item by the total number of motorists in the overall sample (382) and subtracting the answer from 1. The simple process of arithmetic, calculated on the frequency of response to any item, weighed each in terms of their degree of Aggression in order to differentiate between Aggressive acts, for example, 'striking another motorist when annoyed', against only 'making rude signs'.

To illustrate the method of scoring applied, we will take item 55 as an example.

In the response to this item, it was found that out of the total sample of motorists, 309 out of 382 responded positively to 'swearing at other motorists'. As indicated above, the basic score of this item was 1 (as with all other AG and AN items), and the subsidiary score was derived by applying the simple formula:

$$s = K \frac{N_v}{N}$$

Where $K = 1$ (constant)
N_v = Total number of responses to a particular item
N = Total number of motorists in the overall, main sample = 382

or by substituting the respective figures,

$$s = 1 - \frac{309}{382} = 0 \cdot 19$$

The total AG score of item 55 therefore, was

$$1 + 0 \cdot 19 = 1 \cdot 19$$

Each item, in other words, had a raw score of 1, plus an additional score of 1, minus the total sample response to that item (divided by 382).

The reason for having the product of the result (e.g. the result of $\frac{309}{382}$ subtracted from 1 was simply to facilitate a system of calculating differences in the AG or AN context of each item by reducing them to a common factor.

The maximum Aggression score possible, therefore, was 50·96, and the maximum Anxiety score possible was 25·83 (see Appendix III for the score given to each item of AG and AN).

For convenience, scores were arranged into the ten groups shown in *Table 11*.

Table 11

Ten AG and AN score groups (main
study)

Score groups	Scores AG	Scores AN
1	0–5·096	0–2·583
2	5·096–10·192	2·583–5·166
3	10·192–15·288	5·166–7·749
4	15·288–20·384	7·749–10·332
5	20·384–25·480	10·332–12·915
6	25·480–30·576	12·915–15·498
7	30·576–35·672	15·498–18·081
8	35·672–40·768	18·081–20·664
9	40·768–45·864	20·664–23·247
10	45·864–50·960	23·247–25·830

THE INTERVIEW SAMPLE

In Part I we dealt with the interviews. Let us here explain how those motorists interviewed were selected.

Ideally, interviews with all 382 motorists would have given, one assumes, more intensive information than interviews with a smaller number. For practical reasons, however, this was impossible, and a decision had to be made as to which motorists should be interviewed.

Two hundred and fifty-nine, or 67·8% of all motorists, were within ± 1 Standard Deviation of the AG and AN mean scores. Those outside ± 1 S.D. of the mean were found to account for 32·2% of all accidents recorded in the survey. An arbitrary decision was made, to interview a proportion of the latter (123), as they were the ones with extreme scores and/or showed extreme (i.e. very high or low) accident scores.

These 123 whose scores fell on either side of ± 1 S.D. consisted of 35F and 88M. Their respective recorded accidents were:
Female: 14 minor, 2 serious, 0 very serious
Male: 41 minor, 18 serious, 6 very serious
and accident points per person,
Female: 0·51
Male: 1·08
The male accident points per person were on a par with the highest accident points per person recorded (see *Table 18a*, page 114).

For interviewing purposes, however, even 123 were too many, so it was decided to rank their AG/AN scores and to interview: (*i*) 60 motorists, i.e. 30 from either extreme, in order that later comparison might be made, and (*ii*) those motorists who were not already part of either of the two 'extreme' groups and who showed high accident scores.

The 30 'high' extreme motorists consisted of 21 male and 9 female with a mean age of 23y 8m, who accounted for 24·2% of all recorded accidents; and the 30 'low' extreme motorists consisted of 14 male and 16 female with a mean age of 47y 10m who accounted for 1·7% of all recorded accidents.

Additionally, 7 motorists (6 male, 1 female) with high accident scores and mean age 25y 3m were listed for interviewing. These were not in either of the extreme groups.

In this way it was felt that attitudes and opinions would be expressed by motorists with extreme AG/AN scores, also by motorists with high accident scores.

The results of the interviews have been shown in Part I of the book.

7 Findings

Scoring for accidents (reported in the questionnaire) was done simply by allotting three points for 'very serious' accidents, two points for 'serious' accidents and one for 'minor' accidents. It has already been explained that the interpretation of 'very serious', 'serious', and 'minor' was left to the discretion of the person reporting on the questionnaire, and a check for consistency made with the motorists interviewed.

This method had obvious disadvantages which were further amplified by the lack of provision in getting motorists to include, where necessary, the number of each kind of accident in which the subject had been involved. However, in spite of these drawbacks, for the purpose of establishing accident 'trends' the available information in the manner obtained proved adequate.

After all the responses to the items in the questionnaire had been scored by the above method, tables were drawn up from the results obtained to compare differences between the mean scores of the six age-groups within the sample and in terms of male and female scores (see *Tables 12a* and *12b*).

Table 12a

Total AG and AN scores obtained by male motorists in each group of the sample and mean scores as a percentage of the maximum possible score

Age-groups	Total number	Total score AG	Mean score AG	AG mean as a % of 50·96	Total score AN	Mean score AN	AN mean as a % of 25·83
I	77	1,410·580	18·319	(35·948)	510·433	6·629	(25·664)
II	92	1,604·496	17·440	(34·223)	651·154	7·078	(27·401)
III	41	508·722	12·408	(24·349)	263·477	6·426	(24·879)
IV	40	390·188	9·755	(19·142)	203·280	5·082	(19·675)
V	27	240·345	8·902	(17·468)	136·949	5·072	(19·637)
VI	2	9·277	4·639	(9·102)	6·740	3·370	(13·047)
Grand total	279						

Table 12b

Total AG and AN scores obtained by female motorists in each group of the sample and mean scores as a percentage of the maximum possible score

Age-groups	Total number	Total score AG	Mean score AG	AG *mean as a % of* 50·96	Total score AN	Mean score AN	AN *mean as a % of* 25·83
I	36	436·674	12·130	(23·803)	245·946	6·832	(26·450)
II	25	293·406	11·736	(23·030)	201·534	8·061	(31·209)
III	30	290·940	9·698	(19·031)	263·674	8·789	(34·027)
IV	7	68·286	9·755	(19·142)	39·659	5·666	(21·936)
V	4	22·161	5·540	(10·871)	36·700	9·175	(35·521)
VI	1	2·952	2·952	(5·793)	10·284	10·284	(39·814)
Grand total	103						

We find from looking at the above tables that the high scores of both Aggression and Anxiety are to be found in the lower age-groups, i.e. 17–35-year-olds, though the latter group (24y 7m–35y 6m) is slightly less aggressive. While this is true of the male motorists, the female groups tend to have a rather different pattern of behaviour, becoming more anxious in their motoring as they get older. It could be suggested that there is, perhaps, nothing revealing in such information, for surely this is what most people expect as a reasonable development with age; but let us take another look at the tables above.

Let us compare the scores in *Table 12a* with those of *Table 12b*. One obvious difference is the opposite trend in them. It may be noted that male motorists, as they get older, have a significantly similar fall-off in aggression to the female motorist. But whereas the males tend to become less and less anxious as well, the females begin life as motorists less anxious than they become after, one assumes, having accumulated driving experience. Very strange indeed.

This is further indicated when we find that there is a statistical correlation of $r = + 0·58$* between the male AG and AN scores against a correlation of $r = - 0·87$* between the female AG and AN scores (see *Figure 13*, page 103).

Table 12c shows the pooled means of scores attained by the male

* $P > 0·1$ applying Student's t test of significance and α d.f.

and female samples together with the overall mean scores of AG and AN.

Table 12c

Total AG and AN scores obtained by motorists in overall sample within age-groups, and mean scores as a percentage of the maximum possible score

Age-groups	Total number	Total score AG	Mean score AG	AG mean as a % of 50·96	Total score AN	Mean score AN	AN mean as a % of 25·83
I	113	1,847·254	16·347	(32·078)	756·379	6·694	(25·916)
II	117	1,897·902	16·221	(31·831)	852·688	7·288	(28·215)
III	71	799·662	11·263	(22·102)	527·151	7·425	(28·744)
IV	47	458·474	9·755	(19·142)	242·939	5·169	(20·011)
V	31	262·506	8·468	(16·617)	173·649	5·602	(21·686)
VI	3	12·229	6·115	(11·999)	17·024	5·675	(21·969)
Grand total	382						

AG mean score (corrected) = 13·953 (27·380%)
AN mean score (corrected) = 6·737 (26·082%)

Taking the sample scores as a whole without differentiating between the sexes, we have a correlation of $r = + 0.24$ between AG and AN attainments.

This perhaps suggests that the factors of Aggression and Anxiety have to be reckoned with not only in terms of age but also in terms of sex difference.

Retracing our steps for a moment, it may be noted that the similarity between the responses in the main study (see *Figure 10*) is evident once more if we compare the data in *Figures 5* and *6* with our present correlations of $+ 0.75$ and $+ 0.58$ (male) and $- 0.78$ and $- 0.87$ (female). Once again, a small sample in the motoring context appears to be fairly indicative of the kind of data one might expect from a much larger one.

Such differences as exist between male and female attitudes, and how these differences influence accident liability, were discussed in Part I. Let us here take another look at the sample and the distribution of scores within the age-group.

Table 13a

Distribution within age-groups of the number of male and female motorists in each of the ten AG score groups

AG score groups *	Age-groups												Totals	
	I		II		III		IV		V		VI			
	M	F	M	F	M	F	M	F	M	F	M	F	M	F
1	1	4	2	2	3	8	8	2	8	2	1	1	23	19
2	10	10	16	6	14	8	14	1	10	2	1	—	65	27
3	21	9	15	13	13	9	14	3	5	—	—	—	68	34
4	17	9	26	1	8	3	4	1	2	—	—	—	57	14
5	12	3	19	3	3	—	—	—	2	—	—	—	36	6
6	11	1	10	—	—	2	—	—	—	—	—	—	21	3
7	4	—	3	—	—	—	—	—	—	—	—	—	7	—
8	—	—	1	—	—	—	—	—	—	—	—	—	1	—
9	—	—	—	—	—	—	—	—	—	—	—	—	—	—
10	1	—	—	—	—	—	—	—	—	—	—	—	1	—
Totals	77	36	92	25	41	30	40	7	27	4	2	1	279	103

* See *Table 11* (p. 95)

Table 13b

Distribution within age-groups of the number of male and female motorists in each of the ten AN score groups

AN score groups *	Age-groups												Totals	
	I		II		III		IV		V		VI			
	M	F	M	F	M	F	M	F	M	F	M	F	M	F
1	6	5	8	2	7	3	11	—	7	—	—	—	39	10
2	22	10	27	7	9	6	14	4	11	—	2	—	85	27
3	22	6	18	3	11	5	9	1	2	1	—	—	62	16
4	20	10	23	6	10	4	2	2	4	2	—	—	59	24
5	2	1	8	3	2	5	1	—	3	1	—	1	16	11
6	3	4	7	2	—	4	2	—	—	—	—	—	12	10
7	1	—	1	—	—	1	1	—	—	—	—	—	3	1
8	1	—	—	2	2	2	—	—	—	—	—	—	3	4
9	—	—	—	—	—	—	—	—	—	—	—	—	—	—
10	—	—	—	—	—	—	—	—	—	—	—	—	—	—
Totals	77	36	92	25	41	30	40	7	27	4	2	1	279	103

* See *Table 11* (p. 95)

Table 13c

The number and percentage of motorists from the overall sample in each of the ten AG and AN score groups

	AG		AN	
Score groups	Total no. of motorists	% of sample	Total no. of motorists	% of sample
1	42	(10·99)	49	(12·83)
2	92	(24·08)	112	(29·32)
3	102	(26·70)	78	(20·42)
4	71	(18·59)	83	(21·73)
5	42	(10·99)	27	(7·07)
6	24	(6·28)	22	(5·76)
7	7	(1·83)	4	(1·04)
8	1	(0·27)	7	(1·83)
9	—	—	—	—
10	1	(0·27)	—	—
Totals	382	(100·0)	382	(100·0)

Tables 13a and *13b* and their summary in *Table 13c* show that the greater number of motorists (as one would expect in most statistical presentations) conglomerate about the means, which in this case may appear to the casual observer to be very similar, but which are in fact statistically significant in their difference.

Figure 12 more clearly represents the tendency for score groups 1 and 2 to accommodate the greater number of motorists. Positive skewness in the plotted scores may reflect the positive skewness of the sample (see inset *Figure 11*), which we find is made up mostly of the younger age-groups of motorists (17y–24y 6m, 24y 7m–34y 6m, roughly 17–35 years). It may be said that this is a clear indication of the element of bias in sampling methods earlier discussed.

However, also discussed earlier was the lack of precedent in collecting a 'representative' sample of motorists against which to compare one that is supposedly biased. In fact, if assumptions are to be made it is far more plausible for a 'representative' sample (in age-groups) to include a greater number of young people than their older fellow motorists.

A more detailed account was given in Part I, but let us briefly turn again to the differences in attitudes and behaviour between male and female motorists for, it seems, herein lie significant variations that are

Figure 12

AG and AN scores in Tables 13a and 13b plotted as percentages of age-groups within the sample

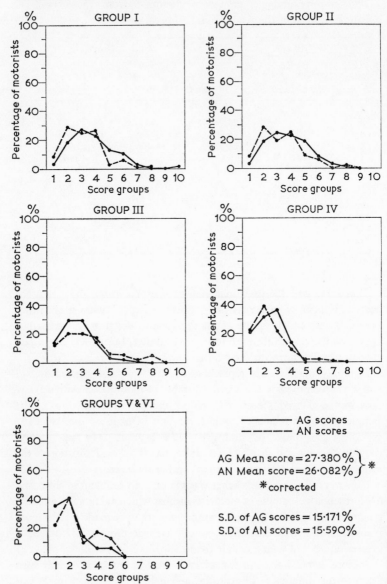

Figure 13
Plotted points of male and female AG and AN mean scores within age-groups

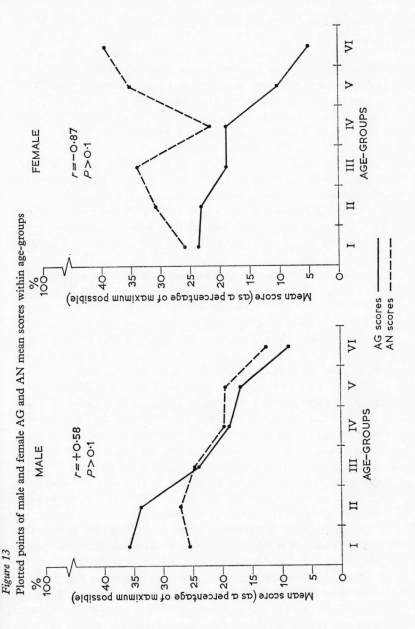

103

discernible as differences likely to cause accidents, potentially, at any rate.

To begin with, within age-groups we are aware that there is a tendency for both sexes to have similar responses to the AG and AN questionnaire items, and that there is a high positive correlation between the groups, i.e. the 17-year-old male responses to the AG items are significantly similar to the 17-year-old female responses, the 25-year-old males similar to the 25-year-old females, and so on.

We have already observed the differences between AG and AN within individual samples (*Figure 13*) of male and female motorists, i.e. the tendency for males to have similar AG and AN scores and for females to have higher AN scores as they get older.

In the curves shown in *Figure 13* we find that the females in age-group IV have extremely similar scores to their male counterparts, i.e. the men in the age-group 44y 7m–55y 6m, and show a rather dramatic drop in the Anxiety curve.

Thereafter the curve, as dramatically, continues its upward trend. The actual mean scores of the male and female motorists in group IV are 19·142% for both AG scores and 19·936% respectively for the AN scores.

One wonders, then, whether at this age in life, no doubt owing to factors other than those mentioned in these pages, there is a coming-together of the sexes in motoring behaviour and attitudes.

Closer scrutiny of individual responses of age-group IV to the questionnaire items shows a startling similarity in their choice of items. We have, for instance, the tendency (reported in the Questionnaire) for both sexes in this group to 'flash their (car) lights at others in anger' (item 74), to 'swear out loud at other motorists' (item 51), to have frequent 'thoughts of' and to 'picture themselves in' accidents (item 57), and apart from becoming apprehensive when police cars are about (item 67) – a fear admitted by the majority of drivers in the various age-groups – a 'fear of the brakes failing' (item 62).

These reported tendencies are not atypical of the motorists in group IV, but it is this age-group in which we find the above-mentioned items, in the order listed, most frequently reported.

These similarities, which are academically interesting though, do no more than make one aware that men and women around the age of 50 tend to behave in a similar manner when driving. We have not, in their defence, any significant figures to indicate that they are any more liable to accidents as a result of behaviour characteristic to their age-group, even though the male accident points per person tend to indicate that the men in group IV are slightly more liable to accidents, compared with women in the same group (see Accident Liability, page 109).

Looking at the sample as a whole, we find the modes of frequency of responses to the questionnaire items are mostly 20, 26, 55, and 68 against the AG items and items 1, 41, 57, and 67 against the AN items.

Most people report becoming annoyed by stickers in others' car windows, preferences for driving fast, swearing at other drivers (under their breath), and profess that they are better drivers than most others. Additionally, there appears to be a preoccupation with the fuel-gauge (even immediately after having had the petrol tank filled), a degree of anxiety professed when in the presence of large vehicles, frequent morbid thoughts of being involved in accidents (no response to this from group I), and – regardless of whether traffic regulations are being broken or not – some apprehension when a police car has been observed near by.

Within age-groups, the tendencies for responses to AG and AN items vary after the initial majority responses common to all groups have been made. Listed below are the most common aspects of aggressive behaviour professed by particular age-groups.

In group I (17y–24y 6m) the more frequent kind of aggressive behaviour professed is that kind most likely to precipitate accidents. There is, for instance, a significantly high response from younger motorists to items which indicate overt behaviour such as (in order of frequency, highest first) 'making rude signs at other motorists' (item 30), 'sometimes taking unnecessary risks when driving for the sake of it!' (the risk) (item 56), 'chasing other drivers (in a car) when annoyed' (item 54), 'disliking others drivers in certain types of cars' (item 65), 'doing something about it (!) if another driver makes a rude sign' (item 44) (odd behaviour when this is exactly what is professed by this particular group, see the first in the list), 'not liking to be overtaken' (item 28), 'being easily provoked when driving' (item 4), 'at times gladly feeling like killing another driver' (item 45), 'fighting with other drivers' (item 8) or 'coming near to blows with them' (item 53), 'trying to edge another car off the road' (item 23), 'making excessive use of the horn' (item 27) and 'driving at other vehicles in anger' (item 38).

In their responses group II show only very slightly less preference for the more openly aggressive acts, and again items 30, 56, 23, and 28 feature high. While there seems to be a slight dropping off of aggressive behaviour after the age of 25, this dropping off is only really apparent when we get to the motorists in group III (34y 7m–44y 6m).

Here we find that common overt aggressive behaviour is mostly indicated by choice of questionnaire items in the nature of 'making rude signs at other motorists' (item 30) and 'swearing under one's breath' (item 55). Generally speaking, the motorist in group III has, by this time, grown out of the phase of displaying 'physical' aggressive behaviour towards his fellow motorists, and is quite satisfied in making only verbal protests when thwarted in the driving situation.

The Aggressive response of the motorists in group IV has been dealt with in preceding pages, though it is worth emphasizing the further decrease of deliberate overt aggressive behaviour by the age of 45 years or so.

By the time a motorist has reached age-groups V and VI his 'aggression' is at a minimum and really only shows as minor expressed annoyances, i.e. a susceptibility to becoming annoyed at seeing 'stickers and suchlike in people's car windows' (item 20), the fact that there are not enough 'rules and regulations in regard to driving' (item 37), 'flashing of headlights in anger' (item 74), seem to be the most frequent expressions of Aggression.

From information gleaned in interviews with some group V and group VI motorists (see Part I) the chief offenders causing annoyance to these older motorists appear to be the younger road-users in groups I and II:

'. . . no consideration shown',

'. . . always cutting in and out [of traffic]',

'. . . no regard for traffic regulations',

'. . . always racing', etc.

However this lack of 'affection' seems to be mutual, for similar attitudes were professed by the 17–35-year-olds towards older motorists:

'. . . creeping along the road',

'. . . always holding up traffic',

'. . . never know what they are about to do next',

'. . . driving without appreciation of road conditions', etc.

Obviously these are gross generalizations made by the two factions, but nevertheless heartfelt attitudes professed by either group.

With regard to anxiety on the roads, we find in group I responses an overall tendency for high anxiety, which rises slightly in the overall tendency of group II, and thereafter drops off, together with the tendency for high aggression, as one gets older (see *Figure 13*, page 103).

Items 1, 41, 57, and 67 are common in their high frequency of response from all age-groups, but responses typical of group I are 'being scared of night driving' (item 40), 'worrying about getting lost' (item 5), and 'becoming jumpy (nervous) when suddenly overtaken' (item 61). Lack of experience no doubt affects such fears.

The overall AN responses of group II suggest that motorists after the age of 25 become slightly more anxious (while becoming less aggressive) before they settle to a progressively downward trend in anxiety in later years. The slightly higher degree of anxiety of group II, in addition to those items characteristic of group I, manifests itself in the form of, 'becoming nervous (guilty?) when other drivers use their horns' (item 9) and 'worrying about doing the wrong thing when driving' (item 59).

The writer makes no attempt to explain the specific cause (or causes) for increased anxiety in this age-group. Such causes would have been more objectively tested had an Analysis of Factors been carried out. This was not done, hence only subjective assumptions within one's own frame of reference may be entered here. No doubt there will be as many reasons as there are readers.

After the increased Anxiety of group II, groups III, IV (already discussed), V, and VI become less and less anxious (as a result of accumulated driving experience, perhaps). In these groups the only frequent tendencies professed for anxiety or apprehension are in situations where 'police cars are about or following behind' (item 67), within 'proximity of large vehicles' (item 41), and persistently 'looking at the fuel-gauge' (item 1). The only assumption one can make on the choice of the last statement of anxiety, especially from information received during interviews with motorists, is the fear of being left stranded should the tank run dry, a fear that is overcome by reassuring glances at the fuel-gauge, often in spite of certainty that enough petrol is in the tank.

So far we have dealt with the age-groups as an overall sample of motorists. In observing the differences between each group in terms of male and female responses, we find that while there is only a very slight difference between the younger male and female motorists, the latter, who tend to be slightly more anxious than their male counterparts, proceed to become increasingly so as they get older (with the exception of group IV, earlier discussed), to reach a maximum peak of Anxiety in their sixties and seventies.

Aggressive behaviour, interpreted by AG scores, on the other hand, follows the pattern of responses made by male motorists in advancing

years, i.e. less aggression as one gets older (a pooled correlation estimate
– where $r = + 0.71$ – between male and female AG scores and $r = - 0.47$ between the male and female AN scores, through the various
age-groups).

At their most anxious, i.e. latter years of group IV and in groups V
and VI, female motorists are apprehensive about almost every one of the
fifteen AN items listed on the questionnaire (see Appendix III for the
complete list).

If Anxiety level alone was a measure of 'accident liability' the
motorists in these groups would have been termed 'most liable'.

The figures of accident points per person do indicate a slightly higher
score for women drivers after the age of 55 years, though this is not
significant, especially as the number of female motorists over this age
in the sample, was relatively small. On the whole these motorists are
fairly accident-free.

It must be remembered, however, that 'not to be involved' in accidents is only a half measure of 'road-worthiness'. More important is the
ability to refrain from precipitating them either by word or deed,
whether deliberately or inadvertently. Here it would seem – perhaps
owing to their high anxiety and consequent over-cautiousness – women
drivers in age-groups V and VI are offenders who, by their lack of
appreciation for particular and varied road conditions, cause more than
just annoyance to the other road-users. By dawdling, driving without
regard to existing traffic speed (though well within traffic regulation
speed), hesitancy, and in some cases (see Part I) being unfortunate
enough just to be old women, these motorists, by antagonizing certain
groups, draw from the more physically able varying modes of aggressive
behaviour.

8 Who causes accidents?

ACCIDENT LIABILITY

From the data given in *Table 14* we find that age-groups I and II account for 58·1% of the total number of accidents reported in the survey.

While on the surface it appears that group III and group IV males tend to have higher accident points per person than groups I and II males, when taken as a sample consisting of both male and female motorists, we find that the total accident points per person (2·90) for group I and II – though only slightly greater – is significantly higher than the total accident points per person (2·87) in the following two age-groups, i.e. III and IV.

Table 14

Showing the number of accidents reported by male and female motorists in each age-group and the accident points per person

Age-group		No. of M & F in group	Accidents *			No. of accidents in group	Percentage of total accidents (rounded)	Total accident points	Accident points per person
			Minor	Serious	Very serious				
I	M	77	32	10	3	45	(19·2)	61	0·79
	F	36	13	1	—	14	(6·0)	16	0·44
II	M	92	49	13	3	65	(27·8)	84	0·91
	F	25	7	3	2	12	(5·1)	19	0·76
III	M	41	23	6	—	29	(12·4)	35	0·85
	F	30	15	—	—	15	(6·4)	15	0·50
IV	M	40	24	4	2	30	(12·8)	38	0·95
	F	7	4	—	—	4	(1·7)	4	0·57
V &	M	29	15	3	—	18	(7·7)	21	0·72
VI †	F	5	1	1	—	2	(0·9)	3	0·60
Totals		382	183	41	10	234	(100·0)		

* 1 point for Minor accidents.
   2 points for Serious accidents.
   3 points for Very Serious accidents.
† Owing to the small numbers, groups V and VI have been combined for convenience.

Before introducing additional data further to emphasize the significant 'accident liability' of the two younger age-groups, we must pause here to explain the derivation of what is to be referred to as the Quartile System.

Even though the data shown in *Table 14* indicated the significantly higher accident liability of two younger groups, a need was felt to try to isolate, if possible, those motorists within groups who contributed high accident scores (see page 12). Were they married or single? Additionally, were they upper-class, middle-class, or working-class people? And finally, and more important, which combinations of AG and AN were responsible for accident-precipitating situations?

In order to answer these questions it first became necessary to draw up tables showing marital status against accident points, S.E.S. (socio-economic status) against accident points, and the Quartile System (not necessarily in that order).

The first two were straightforward. The latter simply was a division of AG and AN scores about the means of each, so that four Block combinations of AG and AN scores were derived. In other words, having the AG mean scores as 27·380% and the AN mean scores as 26·082% (see *Table 12c*, page 99), any higher score than either of the mean scores was High, and any score lower than the means was Low. (Conveniently there was not one score of exactly 27·380% for AG or 26·082% for AN.)

The four Block combinations were therefore as shown in *Table 15*.

Table 15

Four AG/AN Block combinations for use in the Quartile System of differences

Blocks	AG *Score*	AN *Score*	Legend
One (B1)	Above 27·380%	Above 26·082%	High AG High AN
Two (B2)	Above 27·380%	Below 26·082%	High AG Low AN
Three (B3)	Below 27·380%	Above 26·082%	Low AG High AN
Four (B4)	Below 27·380%	Below 26·082%	Low AG Low AN

Having drawn up the basis for comparison in the form of Quartile Blocks, the six age-groups were next distributed in terms of socio-economic classification (*Table 16a*). Criteria for the placing of subjects into their respective socio-economic groups were based on the Registrar General's classification of occupations (GRO, 1960). For convenience,

Table 16a

Distribution of sample into male and female age-groups, socio-economic class groups, and the number of accidents reported in each

Age-groups		AB	C1	C2	D+	Totals
		Socio-economic class groups				
I	M	—	30	38	9	77
		0/0/0 *	12/4/1	17/3/2	3/3/0	32/10/3
	F	2	21	13	—	36
		1/1/0	7/0/0	5/0/0	0/0/0	13/1/0
II	M	9	35	35	13	92
		5/2/0	15/5/2	21/6/1	8/0/0	49/13/3
	F	5	10	9	1	25
		1/0/0	3/2/1	3/1/0	0/0/1	7/3/2
III	M	5	18	13	5	41
		3/1/0	9/4/0	11/1/0	0/0/0	23/6/0
	F	7	10	7	6	30
		2/0/0	5/0/0	6/0/0	2/0/0	15/0/0
IV	M	1	14	18	7	40
		0/0/0	9/1/0	12/3/2	3/0/0	24/4/2
	F	1	4	1	1	7
		1/0/0	2/0/0	1/0/0	0/0/0	4/0/0
V & VI	M	1	9	12	7	29
		1/0/0	4/2/0	8/1/0	2/0/0	15/3/0
	F	1	1	1	2	5
		0/0/0	0/1/0	0/0/0	1/0/0	1/1/0
Totals	M	16	106	116	41	279
		9/3/0	49/16/3	69/14/5	16/3/0	143/36/8
	F	16	46	31	10	103
		5/1/0	17/3/1	15/1/0	3/0/1	40/5/2
Grand Totals		32	152	147	51	382
		14/4/0	66/19/4	84/15/5	19/3/1	183/41/10

* Accident figures, i.e. Minor/Serious/Very Serious.

however, stratification was into four groups only, AB, C1, C2, and D+ (i.e. D's and E's).

Accordingly, it transpired that the majority of the sample motorists were in either the upper- or lower-middle classes, with a trailing-off in numbers of the upper and working classes.

Table 16a also shows the distribution of accidents for each of the four social classes, which is summarized in *Table 16b*.

Here we observe that motorists in the middle classes tend towards a higher accident liability, for the figures show a statistically significant

Table 16b

Summary of socio-economic classification and accident points for each class group

Overall sample	Socio-economic class groups			
	AB	C1	C2	D+
Males number accidents	16 9/3/0 *	106 49/16/3	116 69/14/5	41 16/3/0
Females number accidents	16 5/1/0	46 17/3/1	31 15/1/0	10 3/0/1
Grand totals	32 14/4/0	152 66/19/4	147 84/15/5	51 19/3/1
Accident points †	$14 + 8 + 0$ $= 22$	$66 + 38 + 12$ $= 116$	$84 + 30 + 15$ $= 129$	$19 + 6 + 3$ $= 28$
Accident point per person	$\frac{22}{32} = 0.69$	$\frac{116}{152} = 0.76$	$\frac{129}{147} = 0.88$	$\frac{28}{51} = 0.55$

* Accident figures, i.e. Minor/Serious/Very serious.
†1 point for Minor accidents.
2 points for Serious accidents.
3 points for Very Serious accidents.

Table 17

Age-groups by marital status, with accidents reported and accident points per person

Age-group	Number in group and marital status	Accidents			Total accident points	Accident points per person *
		Minor	Serious	Very serious		
I	89 Single	35	10	3	64	0·72
	23 Married	9	1	—	11	0·48
	1 Other	1	—	—	1	1·00
II	35 Single	18	3	—	24	0·69
	79 Married	38	13	5	79	1·00
	3 Other	—	—	—	0	0·00
III	11 Single	6	1	—	8	0·73
	57 Married	30	5	—	40	0·70
	3 Other	2	—	—	2	0·67
IV	2 Single	1	1	—	3	1·50
	44 Married	27	3	2	39	0·89
	1 Other	—	—	—	0	0·00
V	2 Single	1	—	—	1	0·50
&	29 Married	14	3	—	20	0·69
VI	3 Other	1	1	—	3	1·00
Totals	139 Single	61	15	3	100	0·72
	232 Married	118	25	7	189	0·82
	11 Other	4	1	—	6	0·55
Grand total	382	183	41	10		

* Rounded.

difference between the accident points per person for each socio-economic class group.

One can draw all kinds of inferences and make many interesting assumptions as to why the middle classes (and specifically the lower-middle class) are more susceptible to accidents. But these can be no more than assumptions, for very much earlier mention was made of the numerous factors that influence motoring behaviour (and consequently accident liability) which are doubtless significant, and which have not been included for investigation here.

The reader is at liberty to form his own opinions, based on personal attitudes. No doubt in accounting for 'social' differences as an influence on motoring behaviour one will be tempted to include quite irrelevant reasons; until such time as specific factors are measured, however, subjectivity is unavoidable.

With regard to marital status, mention has already been made of the distribution of accident points (shown in *Table 17* above) and of the lack of statistical significance in the figures suggesting any importance in the influence of marital status on characteristics of driving behaviour.

Next, we proceed to a presentation of the Quartiles of AG/AN Block combinations shown in *Tables 18a* and *18b*.

It certainly appears, looking at the data in the above tables, that both High Aggression and High Anxiety in the motoring situation make for a greater degree of accident liability. The accident points per person shown at the bottom are rather significant and suggest that, in both the male and female samples, combinations of High AG and High AN are to be taken seriously. Indeed, the figures in Block Two show that High Aggression, whether it is combined with High Anxiety or not, is still effective enough in making people more prone to accidents. High Anxiety, on the other hand – when combined even with Low Aggression – is not far behind in its influence on accident liability, so it follows naturally that a combination of Low Aggression with Low Anxiety is the safest in its consequences for contribution towards accidents. Block Four bears this out.

No rotation for factor analysis (normally to be applied in such investigations) was carried out to isolate specific 'attitudes' or 'behaviour' as being causative to accident-proneness, for it was felt sufficient for the purposes of this survey only to investigate combinations of Aggression and Anxiety as a whole without deeper analysis of their constituents.

The tables are self-explanatory and show the distribution into age-oups of the number in each Block.

Table 18a

Male Quartile distribution of AG/AN scores, number of accidents reported, and accident points per person within each of the four Blocks

	Block one high AG/high AN — Accidents					Block two high AG/low AN — Accidents					Block three low AG/high AN — Accidents					Block four low AG/low AN — Accidents				
Age-groups	No.*	Min.	Ser.	V. ser.	Nil	No.*	Min.	Ser.	V. ser.	Nil	No.*	Min.	Ser.	V. ser.	Nil	No.*	Min.	Ser.	V. ser.	Nil
I	24	12	5	3	8	28	13	5	—	13	8	1	—	—	7	17	6	—	—	11
II	29	17	5	1	6	30	18	4	2	6	15	4	4	—	7	18	10	—	—	8
III	9	7	2	—	—	9	6	—	—	3	7	3	1	—	3	16	7	3	—	6
IV	1	—	1	—	—	4	2	1	1	1	9	6	—	1	2	26	16	2	—	8
V & VI	1	1	—	—	—	4	2	1	—	2	6	4	1	—	1	18	8	1	—	9
Totals	64	37	13	4	14	75	41	11	3	25	45	18	6	1	20	95	47	6	—	42
Accident points	37 + 26 + 12 = 75					41 + 22 + 9 = 72					18 + 12 + 3 = 33					47 + 12 + 0 = 59				
Accident points per person	$\frac{75}{64}$ = 1·19					$\frac{72}{75}$ = 0·97					$\frac{33}{45}$ = 0·73					$\frac{59}{95}$ = 0·62				

114

* i.e. No. of motorists in this Block. Some motorists had accidents in more than one category.

Table 18b

Female Quartile distribution of AG/AN scores, number of accidents reported, and accident points per person within each of the four Blocks

Age-groups	Block one high AG/high AN Accidents					Block two high AG/low AN Accidents					Block three low AG/high AN Accidents					Block four low AG/low AN Accidents				
	No.*	Min.	Ser.	V. ser.	Nil	No.*	Min.	Ser.	V. ser.	Nil	No.*	Min.	Ser.	V. ser.	Nil	No.*	Min.	Ser.	V. ser.	Nil
I	5	1	1	—	4	9	3	—	—	6	11	5	1	—	5	11	4	—	—	7
II	4	—	1	2	2	3	1	1	—	1	10	5	—	—	5	8	1	1	—	6
III	4	1	—	—	3	2	2	—	—	—	13	8	—	—	5	11	4	—	—	7
IV	1	—	—	—	1	1	1	—	—	—	1	—	—	—	1	4	3	—	—	1
V & VI	0	—	—	—	—	0	—	—	—	—	5	1	1	—	3	0	—	—	—	1
Totals	14	2	1	2	10	15	7	1	—	7	40	19	2	—	19	34	12	1	—	21
Accident points	2 + 2 + 6 = 10					7 + 2 + 0 = 9					19 + 4 + 0 = 23					12 + 2 + 0 = 14				
Accident points per person	$\frac{10}{14} = 0.71$					$\frac{9}{15} = 0.60$					$\frac{23}{40} = 0.58$					$\frac{14}{34} = 0.41$				

* i.e. No. of motorists in this Block. Some motorists had accidents in more than one category.

115

THE HYPOTHESIS RE-EXAMINED, AND CONCLUDING DISCUSSION

We have seen from the data presented in preceding pages that at least some aspects of the stated hypothesis have been borne out. It has been shown that there is a tendency for High Aggression, whether or not in combination with High Anxiety, to make for greater liability to accidents. In the hypothesis it was proposed that aggression and anxiety when combined were dangerous in their influence on motoring. It was not then known exactly what combinations of the two were most influential.

It has been indicated that the younger age-groups of motorists (I and II) are the most aggressive and the most liable to accidents, that aggression has a greater influence on higher accident liability than has anxiety.

Mention has been made of uncollated data to suggest that, because of their youth, these motorists are apt to pass the driving test most frequently at the first attempt. In the light of information given, this bears out the statement that skill or physical acuteness are in themselves no indicator of good or safe driving.

Finally, marital status is a variable that appears to exert no influence on motoring behaviour, whereas social class does do so.

In Part I we dealt with other points of the stated hypothesis. Once again, let us briefly go over some of the points for discussion.

Most important of all is the question whether or not the sample was 'representative' of motorists and, if accepted as such, how the absence of differences in response between the three sub-samples is to be explained. Criticism on this score would, however, have to meet the challenge of proposing a feasible alternative method of obtaining a representative sample that would satisfy the criteria of age, socio-economic status, and driving frequency. The writer himself adheres to the view that: a sample of only 'known accidents' would have been inept; the sole use of electoral (voter's) registers limiting; a completely self-selective sample academically unacceptable; one in every Nth vehicle to pass a given point only, biased towards the daily motorist, and so on.

A combination of all these with the full expectation of bias, showed none after statistical analysis. Was this because the questionnaire items were such that only a particular response could be given to each? If this were so, all items should have shown either excessive responses or very few. Such was not the case; numerous items having approximately 50% responses only.

One is obliged to assume, therefore, that with the general mass of motorists, driving behaviour, attitudes, and characteristics are much the same; common national driving conditions perhaps leading towards this explanation.

No attempt has been made to gloss over the crudeness of the method of investigation undertaken. It is appreciated that there is ample room for greater sophistication.

Future researches in the field will doubtless have more objective means of studying the behaviour of motorists. But this requires not only time and money in plenty, but at least some basis, however frugal, upon which to undertake a more ambitious approach.

This study was undertaken in the hope that it might provide both the stimulus and the indications for further research in this field.

Appendices

APPENDIX I

Questionnaire

Prepared by M. H. Parry   **C/D AG–AN SCALE**   *10 Crescent Road,*
Hornsey, London N.8.

Your co-operation in answering **all** questions will be greatly appreciated. The aim of this research is to understand more about the driver's attitude to motoring

---

Full name ....   Date of birth ....
Address ....   Sex: Male_____ Female_____
....   Usual occupation ....
     Husband's occupation ....

Please encircle or tick where necessary   All information will be treated as
all appropriate answers   confidential

Marital status
Single   Engaged   Married   Divorced   Separated   Widowed

Education
Primary   Prep   Secondary mod.   Private   Convent/Church   Comprehensive
Grammar   Public   Boarding   Art School   Tech. College   University   C.A.T.
Other

Which newspapers do you usually   Dailies   ....
read?   Sunday   ....

How long have you been driving? ....

Approximately how many miles have you driven? ....

What type of vehicle do you normally drive? ....

Where did you learn to drive?
Privately   Driving School   Forces   Self-taught   Other

Have you ever been involved in a motor accident?   Yes   No
If so was it: very serious   serious   minor

Have you ever been convicted for
Speeding   Not being insured or taxed   Dangerous driving   Other offences

How often do you drive?
Daily   Weekends   Once/twice per week   Less often

Instructions

Listed below are items/statements relating to the behaviour of drivers. Would you please read down the list and put a $\sqrt{}$ in the box of your choice, i.e. that which is nearest your own opinion.

121

Example:

Most drivers wash their cars regularly	☐	☐	Most drivers hardly ever wash their cars

If you thought the first statement to be true you would put your tick in the box near that statement thus √ and so on, down the page. **Please read each item carefully** before deciding. If you feel neither statement to be entirely true, then still please choose the one that is **nearest** the truth for you. This is not a test, so there are no right or wrong answers to any of the pairs, just tick the one that is nearest your own opinion.

There is no time limit but it would help if you completed your answers as soon as possible. **Please do not leave any undone as this makes the whole questionnaire useless.** Your co-operation will be greatly appreciated.

I hardly ever look at the fuel-gauge while driving	☐ 1 ☐		I persistently look at the fuel-gauge while driving
I am never anxious when approaching roundabouts	☐ 2 ☐		I feel a little anxious when approaching roundabouts
There are far too many zebra crossings on the road today	☐ 3 ☐		The number of zebra crossings on the roads today is necessary
I am not easily provoked when driving	☐ 4 ☐		I am easily provoked when driving
I never worry about getting lost when driving	☐ 5 ☐		I worry about getting lost when driving
I never lose my temper when another driver does something silly	☐ 6 ☐		I lose my temper when another driver does something silly
There are more bad drivers than good drivers on the roads today	☐ 7 ☐		There are more good drivers than bad drivers on the roads today
I have been in a fight with another driver	☐ 8 ☐		I have never been in a fight with another driver
If other drivers use their horns at me it doesn't make me nervous	☐ 9 ☐		I become nervous if other drivers use their horns at me
I become distracted if someone talks to me while I'm driving	☐ 10 ☐		I am not distracted if someone talks to me while I'm driving
Non-aggressive driving means better driving	☐ 11 ☐		Aggressive driving means better driving
Hitch-hikers can be trusted	☐ 12 ☐		Hitch-hikers cannot be trusted
Penalties for driving convictions are too severe	☐ 13 ☐		Penalties for driving convictions are not severe enough
I never cut in and out of traffic	☐ 14 ☐		I sometimes cut in and out of traffic
Most drivers are inconsiderate	☐ 15 ☐		Most drivers are considerate

I am usually patient during the rush hour	☐	16 ☐	I am usually impatient during the rush hour
My driving is worse when I am in a bad mood	☐	17 ☐	My mood does not affect my driving
I get annoyed if the traffic-lights change to red as I approach them	☐	18 ☐	I do not get annoyed if the traffic-lights change to red as I approach them
I have never argued with other drivers	☐	19 ☐	I have argued with other drivers
It does not annoy me to see stickers and suchlike in people's car windows	☐	20 ☐	It annoys me to see stickers and suchlike in people's car windows
I am never apprehensive when changing lanes in traffic	☐	21 ☐	I am usually apprehensive when changing lanes in traffic
I did not pass the driving test at my first attempt	☐	22 ☐	I passed the driving test at my first attempt
On occasion I have tried to edge another car off the road	☐	23 ☐	I have never tried to edge another car off the road
If I notice someone in a tight spot I mind my own business	☐	24 ☐	If I notice someone in a tight spot I stop and offer to help
I do not fancy being a racing driver	☐	25 ☐	I would not mind being a racing driver
I like driving fast	☐	26 ☐	I do not like driving fast
I very seldom use the horn	☐	27 ☐	I use the horn a great deal
I do not like being overtaken	☐	28 ☐	I do not mind being overtaken
If my car is not working properly I worry a great deal	☐	29 ☐	If my car is not working properly it does not worry me
I never make rude signs at other motorists when provoked	☐	30 ☐	I make rude signs at other motorists when I am provoked
L-drivers have no influence on me	☐	31 ☐	L-drivers make me nervous
Most people are good drivers	☐	32 ☐	Most people are bad drivers
I drive at the same speed whether I'm alone or not	☐	33 ☐	I drive faster when I am alone
I am usually quite patient at traffic-lights	☐	34 ☐	I am usually impatient at traffic-lights
It is too much bother to stop for someone to pull out, I rarely do so	☐	35 ☐	I usually stop for someone to pull out
L-drivers are usually no nuisance to other drivers	☐	36 ☐	L-drivers are usually a nuisance to other drivers
There ought to be more rules and regulations in regard to driving	☐	37 ☐	There are too many rules and regulations in regard to driving
I have never driven at another vehicle in anger	☐	38 ☐	I have driven at another vehicle in anger

I am not an aggressive driver	☐ 39 ☐	I am an aggressive driver
Night driving scares me	☐ 40 ☐	Night driving does not scare me
I feel anxious about large vehicles when I'm driving	☐ 41 ☐	I am not anxious about large vehicles when I'm driving
I feel less confident in bad weather conditions	☐ 42 ☐	I am always confident, regardless of weather conditions
Pedestrians are usually no bother	☐ 43 ☐	Pedestrians are usually a nuisance
If another driver makes a rude sign at me I do something about it!	☐ 44 ☐	If another driver makes a rude sign at me I let it pass
I have never felt like killing another driver	☐ 45 ☐	At times, I've felt I could gladly kill another driver
I do not find it difficult to control my temper when driving	☐ 46 ☐	I find it difficult to control my temper when driving
If someone turns without signalling suddenly, I do not get annoyed	☐ 47 ☐	If someone suddenly turns without signalling, I get annoyed
I become anxious when committing even a small traffic offence	☐ 48 ☐	I never become anxious when committing a traffic offence
I never feel I am going to lose control of the car	☐ 49 ☐	Sometimes I feel I am going to lose control of the car
I never worry about skidding	☐ 50 ☐	Sometimes I worry about skidding
I swear out loud at other drivers	☐ 51 ☐	I never swear out loud at other drivers
I use the brakes more than is necessary	☐ 52 ☐	I use the brakes only when absolutely necessary
On occasion I have come near to blows with another driver	☐ 53 ☐	I have never come near to blows with another driver
I have given chase to a driver who has annoyed me	☐ 54 ☐	I have never given chase to a driver who has annoyed me
I swear under my breath at other drivers	☐ 55 ☐	I never swear at other drivers
I never take any unnecessary risks when driving	☐ 56 ☐	Sometimes I take a risk when driving, for the sake of it [the risk]
I never have thoughts of, or picture myself in, an accident	☐ 57 ☐	Quite often I have thoughts of' and picture myself in, an accident
If the driver behind has his lights shining in my mirror I do not retaliate	☐ 58 ☐	If the driver behind has his lights shining in my mirror I pay him back in some way
I never worry about doing the wrong thing when driving	☐ 59 ☐	I worry about doing the wrong thing when driving

Most people do not keep implicitly to all traffic regulations	☐ 60 ☐	Most people keep implicitly to all traffic regulations
If I am suddenly overtaken I get a bit jumpy	☐ 61 ☐	If I am suddenly overtaken it does not affect me
I never worry about the brakes failing	☐ 62 ☐	I worry about the brakes failing
I worry that I may knock down pedestrians who step into the road	☐ 63 ☐	I never worry that I may knock down pedestrians who step into the road
Women drivers are no more nervous than men drivers	☐ 64 ☐	Women drivers are more nervous than men drivers
The type of car a person drives does not affect me	☐ 65 ☐	I dislike drivers in certain types of cars
If my car is not working properly it makes me short-tempered	☐ 66 ☐	If my car is not working properly I do not become short-tempered
I never feel apprehensive when I notice a police car about or following behind me	☐ 67 ☐	I feel a little apprehensive when I notice a police car about or following behind me
Most people are worse drivers than I am	☐ 68 ☐	Most people are better drivers than I am
Women drivers are not as good as men drivers	☐ 69 ☐	Women drivers are as good as men drivers
I feel as confident driving whether I am carrying passengers or not	☐ 70 ☐	I feel more confident driving when I have others in the car with me
Bad drivers are usually caught	☐ 71 ☐	Bad drivers usually get away with it
If I find myself in the wrong lane of traffic I stay put	☐ 72 ☐	If I find myself in the wrong lane I cut across, regardless of traffic conditions
I am always relaxed when driving	☐ 73 ☐	I get quite tense when driving
I have been known to flash my car lights at others, in anger	☐ 74 ☐	I have never flashed my car lights at others, in anger
At night I flash my car lights when others have their headlamps on	☐ 75 ☐	I never flash my car lights when others have their headlamps on

K

APPENDIX II

Driving frequencies of motorists in sample

Table 19
Driving frequencies

Age-group	Sex	Daily	Weekends	Once or twice a week	More often	Rarely	N/A	Totals
I	M	56	3	7	6	2	3	77
	F	15	5	8	5	3	—	36
II	M	74	4	6	2	5	1	92
	F	16	—	5	1	3	—	25
III	M	32	5	2	1	1	—	41
	F	21	—	3	2	4	—	30
IV	M	30	3	5	1	1	—	40
	F	6	—	1	—	—	—	7
V & VI	M	25	2	2	—	—	—	29
	F	3	—	1	—	1	—	5
Totals	M	217	17	22	10	9	4	279
	F	61	5	18	8	11	—	103
Grand totals		278	22	40	18	20	4	382
Percentage of sample		(72·8)	(5·8)	(10·5)	(4·7)	(5·2)	(1·0)	(100·0)

Interpretation of AG and AN item numbers and scores

Table 20a
Aggression

No.	Item no.	Legend	Item score
1	3	There are far too many zebra crossings on the road today	1·921
2	4	I am easily provoked when driving	1·804
3	6	I lose my temper when another driver does something silly	1·602
4	8	I have been in a fight with another driver	1·927
5	18	I get annoyed if the traffic lights change to red as I approach them	1·717
6	20	It annoys me to see stickers and suchlike in people's car windows	1·523
7	23	On occasion I have tried to edge another car off the road	1·898
8	25	I would not mind being a racing driver	1·675
9	26	I like driving fast	1·251
10	27	I use the horn a great deal	1·919
11	28	I do not like being overtaken	1·861
12	30	I make rude signs at other motorists when I am provoked	1·696
13	33	I drive faster when I am alone	1·573
14	37	There are too many rules and regulations in regard to driving	1·518
15	38	I have driven at another vehicle in anger	1·942
16	39	I am an aggressive driver	1·843
17	44	If another driver makes a rude sign at me I do something about it	1·827
18	45	At times I've felt I could gladly kill another driver	1·861
19	46	I find it difficult to control my temper when driving	1·890
20	51	I swear out loud at other drivers	1·528
21	53	On occasion I have come near to blows with another driver	1·908
22	54	I have given chase to a driver who has annoyed me	1·772
23	55	I swear under my breath at other drivers	1·190

Table 20a (continued)
Aggression

No.	Item no.	Legend	Item score
24	56	Sometimes I take a risk when driving, for the sake of it [the risk]	1·783
25	58	If the driver behind has his lights shining in my mirror I pay him back in some way	1·835
26	65	I dislike drivers in certain types of cars	1·756
27	68	Most people are worse drivers than I am	1·300
28	72	If I find myself in the wrong lane I cut across, regardless of traffic conditions	1·709
29	74	I have been known to flash my car lights at others, in anger	1·502
30	75	At night I flash my car lights when others have their headlamps on	1·429
		TOTAL	50·960

Table 20b
Anxiety

No.	Item no.	Legend	Item score
1	1	I persistently look at the fuel-gauge while driving	1·342
2	5	I worry about getting lost when driving	1·801
3	9	I become nervous if other drivers use their horns at me	1·822
4	31	L-drivers make me nervous	1·748
5	40	Night-driving scares me	1·849
6	41	I feel anxious about large vehicles when I'm driving	1·743
7	49	Sometimes I feel I am going to lose control of the car	1·880
8	52	I use the brakes more than is necessary	1·756
9	57	Quite often I have thoughts of, and picture myself in, an accident	1·599
10	59	I worry about doing the wrong thing when driving	1·565
11	61	If I am suddenly overtaken I get a bit jumpy	1·793
12	62	I worry about the brakes failing	1·654
13	67	I feel a little apprehensive when I notice a police car about or following behind me	1·434
14	70	I feel more confident driving when I have others in the car with me	1·985
15	73	I get quite tense when driving	1·859
		TOTAL	25·830

APPENDIX IV
Sentence completion schedule

AG sentence completion   AG%

1. 3 The number of zebra crossings on the road are ...
2. 4 For me to be provoked when driving is ...
3. 6 When another driver does something silly I ...
4. 8 For me, fighting with another driver is ...
5. 18 If the traffic lights change to red as I approach them, I usually ...
6. 20 I think that stickers and suchlike in people's car windows are ...
7. 23 In anger, to edge another car off the road with mine ...
8. 25 If given the opportunity of becoming a racing driver I ...
9. 26 For me, to drive fast is ...
10. 27 I use the horn ...
11. 28 When I'm being overtaken by another car I ...
12. 30 In my opinion, making rude signs at another motorist when provoked is ...
13. 33 When I drive alone my driving speed ...
14. 37 The existing rules and regulations with regard to driving are ...
15. 38 Where I'm concerned, driving at another vehicle when angry is ..
16. 39 Aggressive drivers ...
17. 44 If another driver makes a rude sign at me I ...
18. 45 With me, the feeling of gladly wanting to kill another driver ...
19. 46 Controlling my temper when driving is ...
20. 51 Swearing out loud at others is ...
21. 53 To come near to blows with another driver is ...
22. 54 Chasing another driver when annoyed ...
23. 55 Swearing under one's breath at others is ...
24. 56 To take a risk when driving is ...

25. 58 If the chap behind has his lights shining in my mirror I . . .

26. 65 To dislike drivers in certain types of cars is . . .

27. 68 My driving compared with others' is . . . because . . .

28. 72 When in the wrong lane in traffic . . .

29. 74 Flashing headlights at others in anger . . .

30. 75 Flashing headlights at others with theirs on . . .

AN sentence completion   AN%

1. 1 To look at the fuel-gauge frequently . . .

2. 5 Where I'm concerned, getting lost when driving is . . .

3. 9 If other drivers use their horns at me I . . .

4. 31 L-drivers . . .

5. 40 Night-driving . . .

6. 41 When driving near large vehicles I usually . . .

7. 49 With me, controlling the car is . . .

8. 52 The amount of use I make of the brakes is . . .

9. 57 With me, having thoughts of and picturing accidents is . . .

10. 59 With me, to do the right thing when driving is . . .

11. 61 If suddenly overtaken I . . .

12. 62 The thought of my brakes failing . . .

13. 67 If I notice a police car about or behind me I . . .

14. 70 Having others in the car with me . . .

15. 73 To get tense when driving is . . .

References

BERNARD, M. 1952–53. Driver selection in the Paris public transport enterprises. *Z. Verkehrssicherheit 1* (9/10): 418–36.

BINGHAM, W. V. 1931. Management's concern with research in industrial psychology. *Harvard Bus. Rev. 10*: 40–43.

BRITISH ROAD FEDERATION 1964. *Basic Road Statistics*. London: BRF.

BRODY, L. 1941. Personal factors in the safe operation of motor vehicles. New York University, Centre for Safety Education.

CLARIDGE, G. 1965. Personality and driving. In *Motoring and the Motorist*. London: BBC Publications.

CONRAD, R. 1951. Speed and road stress in sensori-motor skill. *Brit. J. indus. Med. 8*: 1–7.

CULPIN, M. 1937. The psychology of motoring. *Practitioner 139*: 213–17.

DAVIS, D. R. 1948. Pilot error: some laboratory experiments. Air Ministry A.P. 3139A. London: HMSO.

DAVIS, D. R. & COILEY, P. A. 1959. Accident-proneness in drivers. *Ergonomics 2* (3): 239–46.

DUNBAR, F. 1944. Susceptibility to accidents. *Med. Clin. N. Amer. 28*: 653–62.

FARMER, E. & CHAMBERS, E. G. 1939. A study of accident-proneness among motor drivers. Medical Research Council, Industrial Health Research Board Report No. 84. London: HMSO.

GHISELLI, E. E. & BROWN, C. W. 1948. *Personal and Industrial Psychology*. New York: McGraw-Hill.

HMSO. 1965a. Commissioner of Police for the Metropolis *Report 1963*. London: HMSO.

HMSO. 1965b. *Annual Abstract of Statistics*, No. 102. London: HMSO.

GREENSHIELDS, B. D. 1936. Reaction time in automobile driving. *J. appl. Psychol. 20*: 353–8.

GRO. 1960. *Classification of Occupations*. London: HMSO.

HÄKKINEN, S. 1958. *Traffic Accidents and Driver Characteristics – a Statistical and Psychological Study*. Finland's Institute of Technology, Scientific Researches No. 13. Helsinki.

LAUER, A. R. *et al.* 1939. Highway Research Board Report (unpublished). Washington, D.C.

LAWSHE, C. H. 1939. A review of literature related to the various psychological aspects of highway safety research. Engineering Bulletin Research series No. 66. Lafayette, Indiana: Purdue University Engineering Experiment Station.

MCFARLAND, R. A. 1957. Human variables in highway safety. *Int. Road-safety and Traffic Rev.* Winter 1966, V (3): 15. (OTA) London.

MORONEY, M. J. 1965. *Facts from Figures*. Rev. edn. Harmondsworth: Penguin Books.

SHAW, LYNETTE 1965. Road safety and the practical use of projective personality tests as accident predictors. *Int. Road-safety and Traffic Rev.* Winter 1966 *14* (1) (OTA) London.

131

132 · *References*

TILLMAN, W. A. & HOBBS, G. E. 1949. The accident-prone automobile driver. A study of psychiatric and social background. *Amer. J. Psychiat.* **106** (5): 321–31.
ROAD RESEARCH LABORATORIES 1963. *Research on Road Safety.* London: HMSO.
World Road News. 1966a. International news review. August, *1* (8): 21.
World Road News. 1966b. December, *1* (12): 28.

Index

Index

accident liability, 99, 108–16
  age-groups and, 109
  aggression and, 20, 113
  anxiety and, 113
  discussion, 116
  marital status and, 110
  social status and, 110–13
accident-precipitating behaviour, 5
accident-proneness, xv, 8, 12, 40, 61–4
accident-repeaters, 8, 64
accident scores, 95
accident statistics, apathy to, 5
accidents, 39–41, 73
  attitudes to, 26
  causes, 109–17
  correct meaning of, 4
  during holidays, 5
  female distribution, 115
  male distribution, 114
  marital status and, 112
  scoring for, 97
  statistics, 3
  use of term, 4–5
  yearly cost of, 10
Aesthetokinetic tests, 62
age-groups, 43
  and accident liability, 109
  aggressive tendencies, 19, 29
  distribution in aggression score, 99–104
  distribution in anxiety score, 99–104
  distribution percentage of sample, 92
aggression
  accident liability and, 20, 113

  attitudes to, 64
  behaviour patterns questionnaire, 13
  combating, 56–7
  forms of, 4
  in females, 75
  in males, 74
  types of, 56
aggression factors in driving, 12
aggression item numbers, interpretation and scores, 127–8
aggression responses, 83, 89
  female, 82
  frequency, 70, 84–5
  male, 81
aggression score, age-group distribution, 99–104
  female, 98
  male, 97
aggressive behaviour, 31–2, 106, 107
  most common aspect, 105
aggressive driving, attitude to, 41
aggressive tendencies, age-groups, 19, 29
alternative choice method, advantages, 16–17
anxiety, 55
  accident liability and, 113
  attitudes to, 64
  behaviour patterns questionnaire, 13
  in females, 19–20, 75
  in males, 74
anxiety factors in driving, 12
anxiety item numbers, interpretation and scores, 127–8